Christ suffered for you, leaving you an example, that you should follow in his steps. I Pet. 2:21

THE
Making
OF A
Model

On Becoming a Living Image of Jesus Christ

R. Larry Scott

THE MAKING OF A MODEL

Copyright © 2021 R. Larry Scott

All rights reserved. No part of this publication may be reproduced, distributed, translated, or transmitted in any form or by any means, including photocopying, recording, or other electronic or mechanical methods, without the prior written permission of the author, except in the case of brief quotations embodied in critical reviews and certain other noncommercial uses permitted by copyright law.

ISBN 978-0-578-85683-4

Unless otherwise indicated, Scripture quotations are from the Holy Bible: New International Version, © 1973, 1978, by New York International Bible Society.

Philip Yancey quotes on pages 33 & 83 are from *Reaching for the Invisible God*, pages 138 & 273 respectively.

Charles ("Chuck") Swindoll quote on page 159 is from *The Mystery of God's Will: What Does He Want for Me?*, page 159.

Cover designed by MiblArt
Interior design & layout by Author Digital Services
Published by Scott Publications

TO MY FAMILY

Evelyn and Sheila

Justin, Jonathan, and Jason

TRULY A GIFT FROM GOD

Contents

Author's Note | i
Introduction | iii
Prologue | v

PART ONE · On Becoming a Living Model

1 – Beauty for Ashes 3

Strategies for Living #1: Three Strings in a Four-String World 15

2 – To Dream Again 17

From My Daily Journal #1: God's Irrevocable Gifts 31

PART TWO · The Perfect Model

3 – When God Became a Man 35

Strategies for Living #2: No Room at the Inn 47

4 – The King Returns to Zion 49

From My Daily Journal #2: Jesus, Only Jesus 61

5 – Joy Comes in the Morning 63

From My Daily Journal #3: Doing the Work of Believing in Jesus 79

PART THREE · Modeling Principles

6 – Modeling the Master Part I 85

Strategies for Living #3: If There Is No God 99

7 – Modeling the Master Part II 101

Strategies for Living #4: From Useless Refuse ... a Masterpiece 117

8 – Designed for Leadership 121

Strategies for Living #5: Gone ... but Never Forgotten 137

9 – The Battle for the Bible 141

Strategies for Living #6: The Tapestry of My Life 157

PART FOUR · The Making of a Model

10 – Modeling the Master Begins at Home............................. 161

Strategies for Living #7: Life in the Trenches 177

11 – Too Hot to Handle 181

Strategies for Living #8: A Sin-City Vacation....................................197

12 – Seeing the Invisible 199

From My Daily Journal #4: In Pursuit of His Excellence 217

PART FIVE · The Model Perfected

13 – The Go-Between Spirit.. 221

Strategies for Living #9: The Mistake of My Life................................237

14 – The Final State... 239

Strategies for Living #10: Thirty Years Down ... and Thirty to Go 253

Epilogue | 257
Appendix | 261
Bibliography | 273
About the Author | 285

THE MAKING OF A MODEL

Author's Notes

The sections headed "Strategies for Living" are from my byline, *Strategies for Living*, appearing weekly in several free local newspapers.

Similarly, the sections headed "From My Daily Journal" are personal reflections from my journal, never planned to be shared publicly, but submitted here for they tell much of my journey toward becoming a living model of the Master.

Some of the works cited herein are in e-book format. Because e-books have no fixed page numbers, citations reference the closest chapter title, heading, and paragraph numbers (where available) to locate the quotation.

Introduction

Writing *The Making of a Model* has been a passion, a drive demanding expression, since the early 1970s. With thousands of outstanding authors flooding the market with many of the issues covered here, however, I hesitated to take on the task of adding another.

I began life as every growing young Christian, full of promise and hope. Adequately trained to take on life's challenges, I determined early on to give my best to model the Master about whom I write. But, great ambition notwithstanding, my journey meandered down a rocky road.

But the journey has not been taken in vain, for the process launched a relationship with Christ that has transformed my world. *The Making of a Model* is about much more than my spiritual odyssey; it is the story of my life.

I am an honest, for real, growing Christian. If you knew me well, you would not wonder why Jesus Christ has become a moving force in my life. He has turned me around, and everything about Him has become of interest to me. Jesus' life, His theology, and His manner of relating to people have been the focus of my study. The Gospel of John, perhaps the most *Christian* of the Gospels, has become my favorite New Testament book. Indeed, I have been captivated by the

Master. And THAT... or should I say HE... is what this book is all about.

Far too often Jesus Christ has become little more than an object of debate. His life has been dissected, analyzed, explained... or simply ignored. The life of this great man, however, is most meaningful, not when it is debated, but *when it is lived*. The Christ of Calvary is not to be discovered in the classroom (or, indeed, in a book). You find Him where you live, in the give and take of the mundane.

I know what I am writing about. I have experienced the good, the bad, *and* the ugly; I have seen both abominable failure and commendable success. I have suffered through days of unimaginable despair, financial collapse, divorce, isolation, and loneliness. I spent fourteen years guiding my 18-wheeler coast to coast, separated from my family, forgotten by my peers, out of the ministry, and convinced that all that was important to me in this life was over.

But God did not abandon me. Often unseen and unrecognized, He was there, gently guiding me toward becoming the man I am today.

I am pleased to tell you we serve a God of second chances, a God who has allowed me to rise from the mire and live again.

And God, I am convinced, isn't through with me yet. I believe the next ten years promise to be the best years of my life, for slowly but surely, God is transforming me into ...

A LIVING MODEL OF JESUS CHRIST!

Prologue

In the early 1970s I attended a Time-Management Seminar in Princeton, New Jersey, sponsored by World Vision. For this fledgling preacher in the opening days of a new ministry in Camp Hill, Pennsylvania, it was a conference made to order.

At a mid-afternoon coffee break, conference chairman Dean Dalton noticed Evangelist Tom Skinner among the conferees. We were honored to have such a distinguished guest in our group, so Mr. Dalton invited him to "take a few moments" to greet the audience.

I had seen Tom Skinner on many a Sunday afternoon on the sidelines with the Washington Redskins football team. He was their chaplain, and I was intrigued by what he might have to say. But what, I asked myself, can a preacher say in five minutes? Interested, but frankly not expecting much, I sat up as Tom started to speak.

"Ladies and gentlemen," he said, "we at Tom Skinner Associates are about the business of just one thing. Whether we are working with the men on the gridiron or in one of our crusades, we have one objective: we are developing, here and now, living models of what we are going to be, then and there. That is our mission." And that was it. Saying little more, he returned to his seat. It took him only three minutes, but Tom Skinner made my day.

Perhaps it was a truth for which my heart had been searching. Perhaps it was the voice of God. But whatever it was, I sat there stunned. The coffee break may have been little more than a brief interlude for others in our group, but for me, it was a moment of truth. I wasn't moved so much by Tom's reference to my status after death, the "then and there," but I was captured by the concept of becoming, in this present life, a living model of Jesus Christ.

Little did I know the process God would use toward making that become a reality in my life. God, I was to discover, would use every facet of my journey to remake me into the image of His Son. No experience would be wasted, no crisis without value. And while I still have a long way to go, I have only recently been able to honestly thank God for the road I have had to travel. Would I want to live my life over again? No way! But thanks to the benevolent hand of my heavenly Father, I am a significantly different man from the person I was that day, better than fifty years ago.

The Apostle Paul tells us that "in all things God works for the good of those who love Him, who have been called according to His purpose" (Rom. 8:28). So why the heartache? On more than one occasion, I have had to ask myself, "Where was God when the lights went out?"

My first remembered encounter with this apparent contradiction came when I was only twelve years old. My father, a missionary with the Assemblies of God, was on his way to a

Prologue

small village in the Andean mountains of Peru when a tragic accident nearly took my father's life. He and Frank Isensee, a fellow missionary, were on their way to a church conference using native transportation. The terrain was so remote and challenging neither was prepared to make the trip in his own vehicle.

At the time of the accident, the truck on which they were riding had come to a stop. The dirt road had been partially washed out, and it seemed impossible to proceed. The driver, however, was not one to give up easily, and he certainly did not want to lose the fare from the two American missionaries.

As my dad stood back watching the action, he wondered whether the truck could navigate the corner. Frank, however, grew impatient. Instead of waiting for the truck to safely round the corner before reembarking, Frank climbed into the back and settled atop the merchandise. Called "roughing it," it was the only way to travel at that time and place in the highlands of Peru. There was no room inside with the driver, so they dressed for the weather and rode on top.

As Frank found a comfortable place to sit, the driver began to slowly ease the truck forward. Suddenly, the edge of the road gave way, the truck dropped off to the right and rolled down the hillside. Unable to jump, Frank was decapitated. In his early thirties, leaving a wife and two small children behind, he had given his life for a noble cause, but, as far as we could tell, without purpose. Nothing good could come from this. Had he waited a few minutes, had the loving God he served prompted him to hold off for just a moment, Frank would have survived the accident. "Sure," says the skeptic, "tell me about your good God."

This was not the only time in the ensuing years that my faith in God's love would be severely tested. I had too often seen things I could not reconcile with what I knew of God. And then, I heard Tom Skinner, and he imparted the insight that put it all together.

Living models! The focus of my ministry was about to experience a shift in emphasis. Indeed, bad things do happen to good people; the innocent do suffer for the guilty. Although God surely hurts with those He loves as they go through times of suffering and pain, He still allows it. And, as always, the big question is: why?

Because, and this is the critical issue, *that's life*. Even when there is no evil intent or an act of sin involved, these things happen. Our children succumb to disease, our marriages go through times of stress, our businesses go bankrupt, and our cars get wrecked. But we carry on, often amid tears, and sometimes, frankly, struggling with unanswered questions.

The Christian life promises no exemption from the usual pressures of daily living. But society needs living models who can show from personal experience, yes, even during times of great distress, the honor that is ours in knowing and serving Jesus Christ.

In 1 Peter 2:21, we read,

> To this you were called, because Christ suffered for you, leaving you an example, that you should follow in his steps.

Yes, *The Making of a Model* is my story… but it is yours as well. We are living models! Fractured perhaps, sometimes struggling, but constantly growing that you and I might effectively emulate the life of Jesus Christ, the Greatest Man who ever lived.

Welcome to the journey. Let's walk it together.

THE MAKING OF A MODEL

On Becoming a Living Image
of Jesus Christ

PART ONE

On Becoming A Living Model

The way I see it if you want the rainbow, you gotta put up with the rain.

~ Dolly Parton ~

– 1 –

Beauty for Ashes
How to Rise Above Failure

The Spirit of the Sovereign LORD is on me because the LORD has anointed me to preach good news to the poor. He has sent me to bind up the brokenhearted… and provide for those who grieve in Zion–to bestow on them a crown of beauty instead of ashes, the oil of gladness instead of mourning, and a garment of praise instead of a spirit of despair.

Isaiah 61:1, 3

IT WAS LATE MONDAY afternoon, July 16, 1984, and I can still remember the dread with which I made my way home from work. Forewarned, I was as prepared as I could be, but the moment had arrived, and I could postpone it no longer.

As I entered the front room of our mobile home, familiar objects were missing, and the place was deathly still. It was to be my first evening as an ex-husband, the beginning of a solitary lifestyle that would last twenty years.

There had been no third-party involvement, no hint of abuse, verbal or otherwise, no drugs or alcohol. I had for years been a caring pastor but a difficult husband. And the chickens had finally come home to roost. A letter on my desk informed me she "just couldn't take it anymore." Twenty-five years of marriage, the dreams of doing something significant in the Kingdom of God, my stature in the community, and my drive to be a man worthy of the admiration of my family all lay in ashes at my feet.

I was destroyed. This was, for me, the end of the line. Finished! My ministry, my reason for being, the source of my self-image, and the drive behind everything I had ever dreamed of doing was now a thing of the past.

What made the experience so devastating was a fundamental conviction that my value as a man was not determined by my stature in the church but by my standing at home. My public image was but a reflection of who and what people *thought* me to be; my family *knew me* for what I was.

But as unbelievable as it seems, God was there. I had not been abandoned.

I. The Positive Side of Failure

Every endeavor, almost without exception, must live with the threat of failure. It is the price we pay to succeed. In marriage, in sports, in business, in ministry, and in politics,

1 – Beauty for Ashes

men and women succeed despite setbacks, opposition, and abominable mistakes.

John Maxwell, in his book, *Failing Forward: Turning Mistakes into Stepping Stones,* makes this critical point:

> The terrible truth is that all roads to achievement lead through the land of failure. It has stood between every human being who had a dream and the realization of that dream. The good news is that anyone can make it through failure. (18)

Examples of this principle abound.

Michael Jordan was rejected by his high school varsity basketball team when he was a sophomore. Winston Churchill lost his first campaign for Parliament. Stephen King's first novel, *Carrie,* was rejected over thirty times before it was published. Vincent Van Gogh sold only one painting while he was alive. Walt Disney was fired from his first animation job because "he lacked imagination and had no good ideas." In 1995, J. K. Rowling had all major publishers reject the Harry Potter script. Henry Ford, at age 36, formed the Detroit Automobile Company, which ended in bankruptcy. Steve Jobs was fired from Apple Computer and then hired back again when NeXT, a company he founded after his firing, was purchased by Apple for $429 million.

And then there is Mark Batterson, lead pastor of the multi-site National Community Church, Washington, D.C.

> When I was in seminary, I tried to plant a church on Chicago's North Shore. I actually created a twenty-five-year plan as part of my master's program. My professor gave it

an A, but God gave it an F. It wasn't His plan. It was mine. I went into it for all the wrong reasons.... Failing at my first church plant attempt was both terrible and wonderful. It was a deathblow to my ego, but that's what set me free.... I discovered that failure is not the end of the world. God was right there to pick me up and dust me off. Failure is not the enemy of success. It's the greatest and closest ally! Failure is part of every success story. (Batterson, *All In*, 42, 88)

I took a calculated risk when I committed my life to establish a new church in central Pennsylvania. Failure threatened over and over again. More than once I questioned my ability to survive opposition and disinterest. I can still recall many days when I was in a blue funk over another family who had bailed and left the church. I soon discovered that Satan will never allow us to succeed without mustering all the forces of hell toward our defeat.

But I survived, Trinity Temple grew, and God gave us a congregation of the finest people any pastor has had the privilege to lead. To God be the Glory!

There is much I could say about the stages through which God leads us toward becoming effective, living models of His Son, but let me summarize. The process toward maturity and becoming like the Master is often so challenging that, but for the grace of God, we would surely fail. But we can rise above the fray and move past our disappointments, lost opportunities, and unfortunate decisions; we *can* model the Master.

It is telling that this is the one area in which Jesus does not serve as our Model. He never failed; He was always right. He fully accomplished the work His Father had sent Him to do.

We are not so fortunate, but it is often in our weaknesses and mistakes that we discover our message.

II. The Courage to Stand Alone

When we determine to take a step of faith, to commit our lives to dream impossible dreams, we may have to do so with little help or encouragement. Sometimes, in fact, we may have to battle outright opposition.

In 1968, my wife and I accepted an invitation to open a new church in central Pennsylvania. We were doing so at the behest of the Assemblies of God Sectional Home Missions Director. On April 1, local pastors got together to approve and ostensibly support our project.

We had just traveled cross-country to answer the call and had every right to expect their enthusiastic support. Of the thirty-three pastors present, however, eleven voted against the project. They knew nothing about me, so it wasn't personal. But they were influenced by a local pastor who vehemently opposed our venture of faith, convinced a new church in the area would have a negative impact on his own.

Sometimes, it seems, we must stand alone, hold steady, and stay on course.

> Nelson Mandela was a principal figure in dismantling South Africa's system of apartheid, later became the nation's president, and was an influential world leader. That was his destiny. But his destiny also included twenty-seven years in prison, of which eighteen involved hard labor and the harshest conditions. His destiny included being beaten and humiliated. His destiny included the harm his actions

brought to his family, and he wondered whether it was worth the cost. (Jakes, *Destiny: Step into Your Purpose*, 143)

We eulogize the Apostle Paul for the great man he was. We sometimes forget, however, that by the end of his journey the New Testament church virtually abandoned him. As he awaited execution, he wrote to Timothy,

> At my first defense, no one came to my support, but everyone deserted me. May it not be held against them. But the Lord stood at my side and gave me strength so that through me the message might be fully proclaimed and all the Gentiles might hear it. (2 Tim. 4:16-17)

And so it has been through the centuries. Many of the men and women we now admire suffered greatly before finally achieving the success for which they are honored. I am encouraged by the fact that God, "Chose us in him before the creation of the world to be holy and blameless in his sight. In love, he predestined us for adoption to sonship through Jesus Christ, in accordance with his pleasure and will (Eph. 1:4-5)."

"To be holy and blameless in His sight" is but another way of telling us we have been called to be like the Master Himself! What an honor!

III. The Strength of our Handicaps

During an open discussion forum at our church many years ago, a young lady I shall call Jennifer interrupted the conversation.

I had just commented on my conviction that God has a place in His Kingdom for every one of us, a ministry of service that can be both rewarding and productive. Suddenly, skeptical and perhaps a bit frustrated, Jennifer spoke up. "And what, Pastor Scott, about me?" I knew her well; it was a good question.

Jennifer, in her late teens, was, by popular standards, unattractive and handicapped. With one leg shorter than the other, she walked with a pronounced limp. She came to church alone and, to the best of my knowledge, had few friends.

My response may have seemed callous and unfeeling, but I chose to address her issue head-on. "Jennifer," I responded, "it all depends on whether you look at your handicap as a hindrance … or an opportunity. Will you allow it to hold you back, or will you use it as a means to demonstrate that God is greater than your limitations?"

The story of Nick Vujicic illustrates the point.

When Dushka Vujicic saw her newborn baby for the first time in 1982, she panicked. 'Take him away," she said. "I don't want to touch him or see him." Nothing had prepared her to welcome a baby, as precious as any newborn, who had no arms or legs. Only a few minutes old, Nick was already discovering life is tough.

In time his mother came to accept him, determined he should live as normal a life as possible. Early on Nick developed a can-do attitude. Using the two toes of his left foot, he was able to shave, answer the phone, and get a glass of water. And routine living skills such as feeding himself, personal hygiene, and getting back up after falling had to be learned. Although he had access to prosthetics, he discovered he did better on his own without them.

When Nick was fifteen years old he invited Jesus Christ to be the Lord of his life. That changed everything. At the behest of a high school janitor who believed in him, Nick began to speak to small audiences. He found that he had an amazing ability to instill in others, overwhelmed with their own handicaps, a determination to succeed.

"You can't always control what happens to you," he would say. "The choice you have is either to give up or to keep on striving for a better life. My advice is to know that everything happens for a reason and in the end good will come of it" (*Life Without Limits*, 12).

That attitude was not lost on a young lady by the name of Kanae Miyahara who had come to hear him speak in McKinney, Texas. She was impressed, and so was Nick. In his words, "She literally took my breath away. I could not take my eyes off her. I could hardly concentrate on what I was saying." The rest, as they say, is history. They were married in 2012 and now have four children: two boys and twin girls.

Early on Nick determined he would not allow his physical limitations to control his purpose and place in life.

The truth is that all of us are handicapped in one way or another. That seems to be the sentiment of the author to the book of Hebrews when he writes, "Let us throw off everything that hinders and the sin that so easily entangles, and let us run with perseverance the race marked out for us" (Heb. 12:1).

We are all limited, "hindered" as the author puts it, and weakened, by circumstances or personality idiosyncrasies that challenge our effectiveness. For the Apostle Paul, his "hindrance" was a "thorn in the flesh, the messenger from Satan, to torment me ... in order to keep me from becoming conceited" (2 Cor. 12:7). In his case it was, I am convinced, a problem with his eyes. For the rest of us, it could be a difficult marriage, a tarnished reputation, a physical ailment, or perhaps an unfortunate decision we're going to have to live with. Life is never ideal and few of us will ever come close to perfection

And the author of Hebrews agrees. We are all beset, he writes, with a "*sin that so easily entangles.*" Every one of us is subject to an area of weakness, a pet and private sin we find difficult to control. So long as we maintain a vibrant relationship with God, however, our predisposition to sin will remain under our command. But if we begin to take God's grace for granted, or if we fail to remain obedient and fully committed to His will, our "pet and private sin" will overcome us and destroy our standing with God.

But that is not how it is meant to be. Whatever our handicap, however tempting our predispositions, God wants to take us just as we are and make something outstanding out of us.

I concur with Erwin McManus when he writes,

> I do not believe anyone is born average, but I do believe that many of us choose to live a life of mediocrity.... The great tragedy in this, of course, is that there is nothing really

> ordinary about us.... [But] here is the painful reality: we will find ourselves defined by the average if we do not choose to defy the odds.... To be above average demands a choice. It requires that we defy the odds.... We can refuse to be average. We must refuse to be average. We must war against the temptation to settle for less. (McManus, *The Last Arrow: Saving Nothing for the Next Life*, 3-4)

Sometimes it is a matter of attitude. Can we accept our limitations? Can we be honest with ourselves and still strive to do something significant for God? Fortunately, self-confidence is not a requirement for service. Those who arrogantly see themselves as "God's gift to mankind" aren't. Pride "goes before destruction, a haughty spirit before a fall" (Prov. 16:18). The call of God, always a challenge greater than our strength, is tailored for ordinary people just like you and me.

Jennifer, the young lady from our church, moved away shortly after our conversation. I lost track of her for several years, and then, much to my surprise, at one of our Sunday services, there she was. Dressed in a Salvation Army uniform, it was with great pride that she introduced me to her husband. He, too, was in uniform, the two of them serving the Lord together.

IV. The Drive to Succeed

Jerry Falwell and I went to Bible College at the same time, in the same city, and within just a few miles of each other. We both took our education seriously, had a favorite place on campus where we started each day in prayer, and graduated with a vision to reach our generation for Christ. The dramatic difference between what he accomplished as pastor of the Thomas Road Baptist Church and founder of Liberty University in Lynchburg, VA, and my own track record speaks for itself.

But God did not let me down. Trinity Temple was well situated to become a force for God in the village of West Fairview. Our sanctuary, decked out with a royal blue carpet and hanging chandeliers, was smashing. Our facilities were adequate for the moment, and expandable when demanded by further growth. Had I recognized it, the summer I resigned could have been a turning point for good in my ministry. But, blinded by the pressures of the Pastorate, and wanting to get on with my life, I did not see it. And so, I quit!

The fact I did so was an indication of how much I needed the maturing process that followed. But God did not abandon me and what I forfeited by leaving active ministry at the height of my career became the means God used for my growth and maturity in the years to come.

Every one of us has, in one form or another, a drive to succeed. For some, it is little more than a desire to exploit life for all it offers, no matter what the consequences. Others aspire to wealth or power or influence or popularity. Where we focus our drives and ambitions will have a direct bearing on the direction we take in life.

For the Christian, our highest honor, and our greatest challenge, is to become a living model of Jesus Christ. "This is to my Father's glory," Jesus said, "that you bear much fruit, showing yourselves to be my disciples" (John 15:8). The Master has given a modern voice to the message He preached. It is heard, and seen, in the lives of men and women just like you and me.

What a privilege it is to serve a God who can take a man from the depths of despair and give him "a crown of beauty instead of ashes, the oil of gladness instead of mourning, and a garment of praise instead of a spirit of despair" (Isa. 61:3).

Thank God Almighty!

– Strategies for Living #1 –
Three Strings in a Four-String World

When Itzhak Perlman, a childhood polio victim, hobbled on stage at the Avery Fisher Hall in New York City's Lincoln Center on Nov. 18, 1995, no one knew that, within minutes, he would have to contend with a major crisis.

Slowly he made his way to center stage and sat down. And then, following his standard routine, he placed his crutches on the floor, released the clasps on his legs, and picked up his violin. He was ready to play.

At some point in the concert, however, things went terribly wrong. A loud noise, like gunfire, reverberated across the arena. One of the strings on Perlman's Stradivarius violin had snapped. The orchestra stopped playing, and in the silence that followed, the audience held its collective breath.

It might well have marked an end to the concert, but not so for Itzhak Perlman. After a moment's pause, he signaled to the conductor to begin again. Continuing to play from where he left off, he improvised with his three-stringed violin with such passion and power it left the audience in awe.

When he finished, the crowd rose and cheered. No one had ever heard such music played from a three-stringed instrument. But the great violinist, undaunted and determined to make the best of a difficult situation, was still able to give his followers a concert they would never forget.

The Making of a Model

Perlman's experience is for me a picture of our relationship with God. You and I are like the Stradivarius, magnificent creations, the crowning jewel of the Master's domain. Until we are energized by the Spirit of God, however, we are little more than inert pieces of spruce and maple. The music is there, but we soon discover that without the control and direction of the Master Musician, we are little more than a three-string instrument in a four-string world.

But we are not alone. Few of us find life ideal or without some challenge to our well-being. Not even the Apostle Paul, second only to Jesus Christ in his influence on the Christian faith, was cut a break. He struggled for much of his life with what I believe was a problem with his eyes. "There was given to me," he states, "a thorn in the flesh, the messenger of Satan to buffet me, lest I should be exalted above measure…. And [the Lord] said to me, 'My grace is sufficient for you, for my power is made perfect in weakness'" (2 Cor. 12:7, 9).

The Apostle finally concluded there was only one way to face the future. "Forgetting what is behind," he wrote, "I press on toward the goal to win the prize for which God has called me heavenward in Christ Jesus" (Phil. 4:13).

Like the Apostle, we may be haunted by circumstances we cannot change. We may feel ourselves to be a three-string instrument in a four-string world. But if we are willing to respect the authority of the Master Musician, amazing things happen. What He can do with simple people, fully surrendered to His will, borders on the miraculous.

– 2 –

To Dream Again

On Reaching for the Stars

"I know what plans I have for you," says the LORD, "plans to prosper you and not to harm you, plans to give you hope and a future."

Jeremiah 29:11

I WAS IN MY OFFICE one Saturday afternoon, listening to the music my wife had on in our living room. Bill Gaither and his Vocal Band were singing and one of their songs brought back dark memories of a time I shall never forget. As the quintet sang, *At the Cross,* an old Christian hymn, I broke into tears.

I remembered well the day I first heard the Vocal Band sing this same rendition. I was eastbound, halfway across Texas in my Freightliner, going nowhere with my life. As the voices of Bill Gaither's Vocal Band emanated from my radio, something electric happened. "At the cross, at the cross where I first saw the light," they sang, "and the burdens of my heart rolled away. It was there by faith I received my sight, and now I am happy all the day."

But I wasn't. Recently divorced from the sweetheart of my youth, I was not enjoying my ride through life. It was a time of trauma, loneliness, and despair. I began to sing with them. The song was well-known, a hymn with which I was familiar from my youngest days.

I tried to harmonize with them but never made it through to the chorus. I wept uncontrollably and, for a few moments, the cab of my truck became a place of divine encounter. God was there. In the stress of the moment, I shouted, "GOD, WHAT DO YOU WANT ME TO DO?" And, although I'm not given to hearing voices, a thought passed through my mind that had all the earmarks of a divine word. "*All I want from you is the gift of a holy life.*" And then, silence.

There were several more hours of driving yet that day but, from that moment on, things changed. I had a new perspective on life; God wasn't through with me yet. That day marked the beginning of my reconstruction and slowly, without fanfare, I began to put my life back together.

But there is much more to this story.

In 1978 I made a decision that has haunted me for the last forty years. At the height of my career, with the most difficult years behind me, I set in motion a series of events from which I am just now recovering; I resigned as Pastor of Trinity Temple in West Fairview, PA.

I was enjoying the faithful following of some one hundred and fifty of God's choicest people and I quit! It had been a long and difficult journey from the inaugural service on Sept. 7, 1968. Launching a new church with no outside help or support is not a venture for cowards. There were times of despair and conflict almost beyond my capacity to handle. But God saw me through, and the future looked brighter than it had at any time during the previous ten years.

I had the support of the congregation, my wife was just initiating broader involvement in our church's music program, and our daughter was in her last year of high school. Leaving Trinity Temple was misguided in every way, for our congregation, for my family, and for me. I still can't believe what I did!

I was over-worked and tired beyond belief. Preaching three times on Sunday, periodically teaching the adult Sunday School class between the two morning worship services, going out with our visitation team on Tuesday evenings, leading our weekly Sunday School Staff meeting on Wednesdays, and then teaching a Bible Study afterwards, all contributed to my worn-out state.

Furthermore, I had a weekly newsletter and our Sunday Bulletin to write. I also balanced the books at the end of each month. To say I was busy was an understatement for sure.

Much of this, however, was self-imposed. I led a competent group of people more than willing to shoulder the load. But I had to be in control; I was a far-from-perfect perfectionist. And, indeed, the program reflected the standards I desired. But it left me exhausted beyond belief and I needed a break. So … I decided on a return to Seminary to complete my education. It seemed right at the time but, as it turned out, it was one of the biggest mistakes of my life.

I have returned often to Romans 8:28. "We know that in all things God works for the good of those who love him, who have been called according to his purpose." I have been reminded that I serve a God who majors in the miraculous, a God who is more than able and willing to work around my failures and errors of judgment and make something beautiful of my life.

Three lessons emerge from the difficult journey that lay ahead.

I. Focus on Becoming Rather than Doing

Our commission comes from the Master Himself.

> You are the light of the world. … Let your light shine before others, that they may see your good deeds and glorify your Father in heaven (Matt. 5:14, 16).

That, for me, has never been easy.

One of my more painful memories stems from a 1983 conversation I had with a fellow Pastor whom I believed to be my friend. "Larry," he said, "are you in ministry to serve God or to serve yourself? Are you serving out of a love for God, or are you just *using* Him to serve your own interests?"

It hurt deeply but I fear he may have had a point. The ministry has always had a bearing on my self-image. Like any other professional, ministers never lose their ambition, their desire for acceptance, or their professional pride. I have been no exception. From my earliest days, I was convinced that success in ministry, as in any worthwhile endeavor, comes to those determined to surmount the obstacles, challenge the opposition, and dare to do something meaningful.

I was the perfectionist ... the one demanding control. That it was a reflection of profound insecurity is no excuse. It was a fatal flaw in my ministry and one that precipitated what I have termed my "wilderness wanderings." God was not committed to my success; He was interested in me. Self-centered ambition had impacted my spiritual focus. My weaknesses and immaturity demanded shock therapy and God was about to get my attention as He could have in no other way.

I have been involved in a life-long spiritual battle. Satan took my fear of failure, my reaction to rejection, the temptation to blame myself for ignorant mistakes, and the shame that followed ... to derail the work God initiated in my life.

But God did not give up on me. In His goodness and grace, He had a response for every area in which I struggled. For failure, God offered love; for rejection, God offered reconciliation; for sin, God offered forgiveness; for shame, God made me a new creation in Christ.

I am still a work in process. While I will continue to evolve and develop my walk with God, I am pleased to tell you I have come a long way. I am a different man from who I was just twenty years ago. In the words of the prophet Joel, God has, indeed, "restored the years the locust has eaten" (Joel 2:25).

II. Welcome God's Directives

Being a living model of Christ Jesus, then, is not a mantra; it represents the commitment of my life. Jesus set the pattern I am to follow. It allows for no excuses, no exceptions, and no compromises. I am called to become a living model of Jesus to my generation. When people see me, they are meant to see Jesus. And *that* is an awesome responsibility.

God's primary means of communicating His will is through His Word. "I have hidden your word in my heart," wrote the Psalmist, "that I might not sin against you. … Your word is a lamp to my feet and a light for my path" (Ps. 119:11, 105).

I believe the Bible is the inerrant, inspired Word of God and I want to go on record in stating a core conviction: the Scriptures are the full and final revelation of God. Our understanding of the Father, the deity of our Lord, the work of the Holy Spirit, and the means to a growing, satisfying relationship with God are all outlined in His Word. "Blessed is the man," writes the Psalmist, whose "delight is in the law of the LORD and on his law he meditates day and night" (Ps. 1:1-2).

In my day-to-day walk, however, there are a host of circumstances in which the Word does not give me a clear indication of how I should proceed. For these God has given me common sense, experience, the advice of knowledgeable friends and professionals, and an active conscience. He leaves it to me to apply each as the circumstances demand. And I am not overlooking the powerful work of the Holy Spirit, guiding my life "into all truth" (John 16:13). We will deal with that in Chapter 13.

But in my experience, God has most generally "spoken" to me, not in a word, an impression, or a dream, but in "circumstantial evidence." I am amazed at how often the give and take of life has come together to make His will clear and unmistakable. When the timing is right, everything falls into place.

This was never truer than when Evelyn I decided to remarry. We each felt it was God's will for our lives but, as you can expect, we entered remarriage with serious misgivings. It has been to our strength that God honored our commitment to Him and to each other and verified our decision in a remarkable way.

I owned a forty-foot Hunter Legend sailboat on which I had been living for the previous seven years. We had decided to sell the boat and move to New Hampshire to be close to our family. But with thousands of boats on the market, I faced the prospect with uncertainty.

We traveled to Poulsbo, Washington in mid-June 2004 and got the boat ready for sale. Once ready, we put it on the market. It sold within a week and at a fair price. We came back to New Hampshire, purchased a house, set up our home and my office with new furniture, and settled in by October 1, debt-free!

When God chooses to move, circumstances often coalesce to bring about change in an apparently coincidental way. Things fall into place, sometimes in a way that borders on the miraculous.

It is equally true, however, that there have been times when nothing fits ... when God has indicated an unmistakable "No!" to my plans. For me that has always been a tough call; I tend to stay on course and plow on through.

This was never more evident than my experience at the Ashland (OH) Seminary following my resignation from Trinity Temple.

I had chosen the Seminary due to the strength of their graduate program in counseling. Two options were open to me: Traditional Counseling or Hospital Chaplaincy. I chose to pursue study in traditional counseling and, with my classmates, was anticipating a two-year internship at the Cleveland Psychiatric Institute in Cleveland, Ohio, beginning with our third year of study.

At the end of our second year, a list was posted of those authorized to intern at the Institute in the fall. I could not believe what I saw. Of all my classmates, my name was the only one not on the list. I was devastated. I checked with the Director of Counseling and he couldn't, or wouldn't, explain why I had been the only one not approved. On appeal, however, I was allowed into the program and over the next two years, completed my degree.

Had I accepted what at the time was a major setback to my plans I would have had to wait through the next school year and then could have enrolled in the Seminary's Hospital Chaplaincy program. Only later did I discover that traditional counseling, part science, and part intuition, did not fit my personality. I would, however, have made an excellent hospital Chaplain. I cannot imagine how different my future would have been had I taken this change of plans as coming from the hand of God.

There are two issues at work here.

On the one hand, modeling the Master demands a commitment that refuses to give up. The forces of hell are determined to destroy us, and except for the grace and power of God, we are doomed to failure. There are times when we must stay the course, fight hell with every weapon at our disposal, and believe God to accomplish the impossible.

> Humble yourselves, therefore, under God's mighty hand, that he may lift you up in due time. Cast all your anxiety on him, because he cares for you. Be self-controlled and alert. Your enemy the devil prowls around like a roaring lion looking for someone to devour. Resist him, standing firm in the faith (1 Pet. 5:8-9).

On the other hand, there are times when failure may be divinely ordained. Our commitment to honor God in all that we do doesn't mean we will always succeed in our carefully developed plans. God may have something different in mind.

III. Dream Impossible Dreams

Our weaknesses and misgivings notwithstanding, nothing should be allowed to hold us back from attempting the

The Making of a Model

apparently impossible in the service of our Lord. We serve a great and powerful God and He is anxious to demonstrate His greatness through human beings just like you and me.

The history of what came to be known as the Los Angeles *Dream Center* is a classic case in point.

Matthew Barnett came to Los Angeles with a lofty dream: to open a new church in the City of Angels. It didn't happen. The drive to emulate his father, the successful pastor of a mega-church in Phoenix, AZ, was not to be.

As Matthew was walking through Echo Park God gave him a new vision: to establish a ministry to the lost and hurting in downtown Los Angeles. It would not be a conventional church. His dream was to establish a "hospital" for the hurting, a place of physical, emotional, and spiritual healing for those in desperate need.

Within just a mile of downtown Los Angeles, Matthew started canvassing door-to-door, asking people if they needed anything. The Center reached into the community, beginning with an outside gym in the church parking lot. The neighborhood soon realized this would be a very different kind of church.

With remarkable faith in God and a love for God's people, Matthew Barnett was driven by a passion for the downtrodden in central Los Angeles. Like the Psalmist, "My heart was hot within me, while I was musing the fire burned" (Ps. 39:3). And then he learned the Queen of Angels Hospital, owned by the Catholic Church, was up for sale.

Reality said, "Don't be a fool!" Faith said, "Why not?"

They were seeking to sell it for $25 million and an offer was already on the table from Paramount Studios for $15 million. They made an offer of $3.9 million without mentioning they actually only had $30,000 in the bank.

> The nuns accepted their bid with one stipulation—the mortgage had to be paid off within eighteen months. The pressure was on. Matthew and [his father] Tommy morphed into fund-raising roadrunners. For the next year and a half, they made phone calls, they traveled, and they talked to anyone who could help. At the eleventh hour, which seems to be God's favorite time, the last $2 million came through. The deadline was only a few days away (Barnett, *willing to walk on water*, 82-83).

I faced a similar crisis three years into our ministry at Trinity Temple. Although much more modest in scale, it was just as critical to our future.

I still remember the desperation I felt when the American Legion informed us we had but a few months to vacate the building that had served as our place of worship for the previous two years. We had searched for a permanent home for our congregation but to no avail. It is fine to talk of great faith when the sun is shining but I must admit that, for me, it was a crisis and a nightmare.

Through a series of events I can no longer reconstruct, Trinity Temple acquired a small but lovely Methodist-Episcopal church building in West Fairview, PA. Complete with a working belltower and irreplaceable stained-glass windows, it was perfect for our needs. God came through at just the right time and you would be hard-pressed to find a lovelier worship sanctuary. We installed royal blue carpeting, a floor-to-ceiling light-blue set of drapes behind the platform, set off by front-to-back golden chandeliers. Outstanding! Trinity Temple was back in business.

Next to our property was a two-story, all-brick school building the district had abandoned, and it came on the market. The bottom-line asking price was $13,000, an unbelievable price for the size of the building but for our small congregation of some 80 people, a genuine challenge to our faith. We prayed about it and I invited the congregation to join me in a true venture of faith and offered $13,000. I held my breath — or perhaps, more correctly, I stopped breathing — as I came to the board meeting in charge of the sale. We were the only bidders! Trinity Temple was in business again.

It is amazing what God can do when he finds willing hearts. One of the hidden "stories" involved in raising the $13,000 (which we were able to secure by the day of settlement) was that one of our teenagers had a penny-bank he had kept for several years toward the day he would purchase his first automobile. He gave it all, better than $100 worth of pennies! Within just a few years God honored that commitment and called him into full-time ministry. He is, as of this writing, serving as the Associate Pastor of a church in Hong Kong. In God's Kingdom, a willing sacrifice never goes unrewarded.

Venture to do great things for God. He is still able to do the apparently impossible for those who dare to trust Him. The call to model the Master will seldom be equal to our strength but God does not operate within our comfort zone. He challenges us to a walk of faith that demands His intervention, or we fail.

Dream impossible dreams!

And now, with my personal story as a background, we turn, where we must, to the Person of Jesus Christ. How He lived, what He taught, and why we believe He was the Son of God is primary to this discussion. If that foundation, which I will build in the next three chapters, isn't valid, everything that follows is bogus.

Jesus, a man *in every sense of the word*, was the eternal Son of God. His ministry was without parallel, a majestic and supernatural exercise worthy of His deity. Jesus may have looked like a peasant, walked like a peasant, and lived like a peasant, but common He was not. In his final words with Jesus, just before His sentencing, Pilate declared, "You are a king, then!" Jesus answered, "You are right in saying I am a king (John 18:37).

It is telling that Jesus was so ordinary not even His family believed in Him until after the resurrection. Appearances to the contrary, however, He was Majesty in human form ... the Sovereign God in peasant dress ... the Eternal One in tunic and sandals.

No better description of Him can be given than that penned by the Apostle John. At the end of the ages, when Jesus has returned to earth and been crowned with the Majesty that is His due, He will no longer be seen as the humble rabbi from Nazareth.

Coming out of his mouth is a sharp sword with which to strike down the nations. 'He will rule them with an iron scepter.' He treads the winepress of the fury of the wrath of God Almighty. On his robe and on his thigh he has this name written: King of Kings and Lord of Lords (Rev. 19:14-15).

Unrecognized and unheralded except by a few of His faithful followers, Jesus was every bit of that even during His sojourn on earth. He relinquished, as we shall see, the prerogatives of deity, but He was then, is now, and shall forever be: Jesus the Christ, King of Kings and Lord of Lords!

– From My Daily Journal #1 –
God's Irrevocable Gifts

For God's gifts and his call are irrevocable. Rom. 11:29

That was true for Israel … and it is true for me.

Israel walked away from God … crucified their Messiah … and suffered horrendously because of it … but God's call and His plan for them was not to be negated. Thwarted, perhaps, delayed and postponed, but still due to be fulfilled in its proper time. God, it seems, has never allowed sin and man's intransigence to destroy His objectives. Israel will still see the day when their Messiah will reign to their glory.

And so it is with me. Presupposing that my calling was genuine … and if it wasn't God has certainly honored a willing heart … but granting that God placed His blessing on this fractured life to honor and represent Him … His call, His gifts, are irrevocable, or as per 2 Cor. 7:10 (the only other place in the NT where this word is used) *without regret.*

God, I am pleased to note, is greater than even our failure and our sin. All things do, indeed, work "for the good of those who love him, who have been called according to his purpose" (Rom. 8:28) … and surely that is true in my case.

Having no clue at this point where my life is headed or how it will eventually conclude, it is imperative that I see my remaining days within the light of eternity. God has called me unto Himself ... He has given me a heart for His truth ... He has drawn me to His son ... He has filled me with His Spirit ... and notwithstanding my personality weaknesses, He has brought me to this point to continue my search for Him and my quest for His very best.

And *that* is something He will honor ... and whatever my public ministry I will continue to seek Him until He either opens up the opportunity for a final period of sharing my discoveries ... or calls me home to enjoy the fruits of a life wholeheartedly dedicated to know Him.

PART TWO

The Perfect Model

*Jesus gives God a face,
and that face
is streaked with tears.*

~ Philip Yancey ~

– 3 –

When God Became a Man
Heaven's Perfect Model

*The Word became flesh and lived for a while among us.
We have seen his glory, the glory of the one and only Son,
who came from the Father, full of grace and truth.*

John 1:14

THE THUNDERING VOICE of the prophet could be heard reverberating across the encampment. This man was on a mission! He had something to say and everyone had better listen!

No diplomat this one, and it was clear he wasn't out to win any friends. "You brood of vipers, who warned you to flee from the coming wrath? Produce fruit in keeping with repentance" (Matt. 3:7-8). Harsh but honest, John the Baptist had a message that resonated with his audience. Israel had waited

The Making of a Model

four hundred years for a prophet who would speak for God, and they were impressed. Could this be the Messiah?

Then one afternoon, alone and unassuming, a stranger approached. Typical of other young men coming out of Galilee, no one paid Him much attention. But this man was more than He seemed. This one was majesty in peasant dress, Almighty God in human form. The Messiah had arrived!

We aren't given the details, but in my imagination, I see Jesus standing at the back of the crowd, listening with interest. And then, when there was a break in the action, He decided it was time to make Himself known.

"Hi, John. I'm your cousin, Jesus. Can't tell you how pleased I am to finally meet you!" John, one can imagine, must have been speechless for a moment and then regained his composure. "You know, Jesus, I've been looking forward to meeting you, too. But, frankly, you aren't what I expected."

How ever it actually transpired, that quiet meeting beside the Jordan River proved to be a defining moment for both Jesus and John. For John it was the beginning of the end, his mission as the forerunner to the Messiah, complete. Within the next two years he would be executed by King Herod.

But for Jesus, this was His moment of truth, the day for which He had been preparing for some thirty years. Although the sinless Son of God did not need to be baptized, He felt it necessary to identify with the society He had come to save. "Let it be so now," He said to a reluctant John. "It is proper for us to do this to fulfill all righteousness" (Matt. 3:15).

But this was no cleansing ritual. Jesus' baptism was an induction ceremony, a royal commission, sanctioned by the Holy Spirit and ratified by the voice of God. "As soon as Jesus was baptized … a voice from heaven said, 'This is my Son, whom I love; with him I am well pleased" (Matt. 3:16-17).

No one, however, including John, understood what was going on. This young rabbi from Nazareth didn't look a bit like the powerful personality they were expecting.

Some time later, reflecting on all that was happening to both him and Jesus, John could take it no more. He understood the role he had been called to play, and he had been reassured by Jesus, but nothing squared with what he and his people had been expecting. To settle the matter, he sent some of his disciples to Jesus on a fact-finding mission. "Are you the one who was to come, or should we expect someone else?" Jesus replied, "Go back and report to John what you hear and see. The blind receive sight, the lame walk, those who have leprosy are cured, the deaf hear, the dead are raised, and the good news is preached to the poor" (Matt. 11:3-5).

That settled it for John, but others remained skeptical. Jesus was not the Messiah they were expecting. They wanted a spokesman, a military man, a brilliant tactician, someone to lead them in revolt against Rome. When they found He could heal the sick and feed the multitude there was a temporary groundswell, but it did not last. When the people found He was not going to cater to their selfish interests they abandoned Him and left Him to the mercy of the religious establishment.

Neither His family nor His disciples understood Jesus' mission until after the resurrection. And it wasn't until the Apostle Paul wrote to the Philippians that the church got a clear definition of what Jesus' life and ministry had been all about.

> Your attitude should be the same as that of Christ Jesus: Who, being in very nature God, did not consider equality with God something to be grasped, but made himself nothing, taking the very nature of a servant, being made in human likeness. And being found in appearance as a man, he humbled himself and became obedient to death—even death on a cross! (Phil. 2:5-8).

I. Jesus was "in Very Nature God"

Jesus looked to be a young Galilean, a journeyman carpenter, a rabbi without formal training. But Jesus was more, much more, than that, and we are fortunate the Apostle Paul was finally able to figure it out and put it in terms we could understand.

Christ Jesus, he writes, "being in the form of God ... made himself of no reputation, and took upon him the form of a servant (Phil. 2:6-7, KJV). Humble and unassuming He may have been but Jesus was, in the fullest sense of the word, God!

> The same Greek word rendered 'form' (morphe) is used both times. Paul here draws a contrast between Jesus' heavenly mode of existence, in which he had 'the form of God,' and his earthly mode of existence, in which he had the 'form of a slave.' ... It's safe to say that it indicates a form that fully and accurately corresponds to the being that underlies it. If we think of form as an exact replica or rather, as identical to the

original, we get a good sense of what it means here (Komoszewski, *Reinventing Jesus*, p. 185).

For the early church, Jesus' prior existence in the *form of God* meant He was characterized by what was essential to being God. In form, he existed, before His birth in the mode in which the essential being of God expresses itself. It was not that He was like God but really not. On the contrary, He was God in human flesh, possessed of the divine substance of deity.

Jesus did not consider equality with God something to be "grasped, but instead made himself nothing." The word translated *equality, isa,* is often translated *the same as,* or *alike.* Paul was convinced that Jesus, although appearing in the form of a servant, was in essence and being, God.

> Christ came "in the form of a slave," that is, by his "coming to be in the likeness of human beings." ... The word [likeness] is used primarily because of Paul's belief ... that in becoming human Christ did not thereby cease to be divine. ... Thus he came in the "likeness" of human beings, because on the one hand he has fully identified with us, and because on the other hand in becoming human he was not "human" only. He was God living out a truly human life (Fee, *Philippians*, 213).

Jesus was divine, and He never ceased being God, even in the final hours of His life. What happened at the cross was not the loss of deity, but a pause, a break in the unity and oneness of the Godhead. "My God, my God, why have you forsaken me" (Matt. 27:46) reflected an interruption in the harmony that had existed between the three persons of the Godhead throughout eternity. God abandoned by God is a tragedy beyond our comprehension. It is the price heaven paid for our redemption.

II. Jesus Assumed the Form of a Servant

As per the Greek text, "Jesus *emptied himself,* taking the form of a servant, being made in the likeness of men" (Phil. 2:7, KJV). The issue here is the extent to which Jesus did "empty himself" of the essence of deity. There has always been a question of whether Jesus was a *deified* man or a *humanized* God.

There were times when He seemed to be quite human. As recorded in Mark 13:32, He professed ignorance as to the time of the *parousia*, the second coming. And then there was that time in Nazareth when "he could not do any miracles there, except lay his hands on a few sick people and heal them. And he was amazed at their lack of faith" (Mark 6:5-6).

There were, however, other times when he demonstrated amazing power. Three times he raised the dead, and twice he fed several thousand men and their families from a young man's lunch. On a number of occasions, He demonstrated his authority over demonic possession. He turned water into wine, quieted storms, and walked on water. Never before, and never since, has this world seen a man demonstrate the power of God as did Jesus.

But in taking on the "form of a servant," Jesus exchanged one form of existence for another. "But he made himself nothing, taking the very nature of a servant" (Phil. 2:7, NIV), and laid aside the use of His attributes as God to fully identify with man.

Joni Eareckson Tada, a paraplegic since a diving accident when she was 17, has a unique perspective on the self-emptying of our Lord.

> When you study the life of Jesus, you have to stop and consider that although our Savior did not have a physical disability per se, He did handicap Himself when He came to earth. ... [T]he dictionary defines "handicap" as any difficulty that is imposed on a superior person so as to hamper or disadvantage him, making that person more equal with others. Certainly, if we use that definition, then Jesus was handicapped. ... He emptied Himself, taking the very nature of a servant. Talk about handicaps! Can you imagine a greater one? To be God on one hand, and yet to make Himself nothing! (*A Place of Healing*, 203).

Jesus, in surrendering the prerogatives of deity, assumed all that we mean by being human. So typical was He that His family, those who had been with Him from His earliest days, saw Him as nothing more than an older brother and son. He developed as a normal child, maintained the limitations typical to a first-century Nazarene, and did nothing to counter family attitudes. He functioned as a man, albeit a man under the direction of the Holy Spirit, right up until his final moments on the cross. Only then was His "nature as a servant" finally and gloriously, finished!

III. Jesus was Made in Human Likeness

Our Lord's *likeness* was real, not a make-believe copy of what it means to be a man. This likeness did not express the whole of His being, for He was much more than "just another man." But insofar as this likeness speaks of His human nature, He was an authentic and genuine man. How Jesus could be fully God (and thus bring the glory of the Godhead to the human family) and be fully man (and thus bring the sin of the human family before God) is beyond comprehension.

> The Son of God became the Son of Man in order that He might be an [sic] High Priest. ... Because of the perfect union between His two natures, the Lord Jesus is "a merciful and faithful High Priest": "merciful" man wards, and "faithful" God wards.
>
> The whole context shows us His qualification for this stupendous work which none but He could have performed. First, He was Himself "the Son," the brightness of God's glory. ... Thus it was the dignity or Deity of His person which gave such infinite value to His work. Second, His moral perfection as Man, loving righteousness and hating iniquity (1:9) thus fulfilled every requirement of the law (Pink, *Hebrews*, 144, 148).

In the justice of God, only a man could assume sin's penalty for man. "It is impossible for the blood of bulls and goats to take away sins" (Heb. 10:4). Jesus was God's answer to a dilemma that could have been resolved in no other way.

I make a point of Jesus' manhood for there are times when some might question our call to emulate the Master because He was divine. Indeed, He was, but He lived and functioned as any other man, and what He was able to do, in that capacity, we have every reason to believe we can duplicate if we follow in His footsteps. In short, Jesus identified with us that we might identify with Him.

In Hebrews 2:17-18, we are told,

> For this reason he had to be made like his brothers in every way, in order that he might become a merciful and faithful high priest in service to God, and that he might make atonement for the sins of the people. Because he himself suffered when he was tempted, he is able to help those who are being tempted.

The writer to the Hebrews summarizes our discussion very well and it allows me to highlight two convictions.

First, Jesus accomplished his mission without exercising the privileges that were due Him as the Son of God. He never ceased being God, but, as when He refused to change a stone into bread following his 40-day fast, He chose to live and function as a man. Except for our sinful nature and our self-centered manner of life, Jesus identified with humanity in every way. We have no record of Him taking a bath or having to look for a restroom, but He lived and functioned as a typical man of His generation.

Jesus not only identified with the human family, He also established the pattern He meant for us to follow. We must not minimize Jesus' status as the promised Messiah nor overlook the special role He played as the divine Son of God. But I do believe Jesus meant what He said when He told His disciples,

The Making of a Model

> I tell you the truth, anyone who has faith in me will do what I have been doing. He will do even greater things than these, because I am going to the Father. And I will do whatever you ask in my name, so that the Son may bring glory to the Father (John 14:12-13).

Peter follows this up when he writes, "Christ suffered for you, leaving you an example, that you should follow in his steps" (1 Pet. 2:21).

We *can* model the Master, yes, even in the miraculous dimensions of His life.

Follow the book of Acts and we find the supernatural was also evident in the ministry of the disciples. "The apostles performed many miraculous signs and wonders among the people" (Acts 5:12). Peter was miraculously released from prison when, following his arrest by a jealous high priest, an "angel of the Lord" led him to freedom through locked prison gates (Acts 5:19). In Joppa, Peter was instrumental in bringing Tabitha back to life (Acts 9:40). In Acts 28:9, Paul was on the island of Malta on his way to Rome, and after praying for Publius' father and healing him, "the rest of the sick on the island came and were cured."

And that brings me to a second conviction.

The miraculous dimension of Jesus' ministry must be credited, not to the fact of his deity, but the power of the Holy Spirit. Indeed, the word "Christ," the "anointed" one, tells us the source of His power.

> He became [sic] in the likeness of men. It was all voluntary on His part. And, as a man on earth, He chose to be guided by the Holy Spirit. He daily received from the Father,

through the Word of God, the instruction which it became Him, as a man, to receive. His mighty works of power were not wrought by His own divine omnipotence alone. He chose that they should be wrought in the power of the Holy Spirit (Ironside, *Philippians*, 42).

I find this understanding essential to my faith if I am to believe, consistent with the theme of this book, that God has called us to become living models of the Master. The fact Jesus was divine does not deny us the privilege to model Him in every aspect of His life and ministry. What He did, He did in the power of the Holy Spirit and the Holy Spirit is still at work. God's power is unlimited, and God can, and still does, move in supernatural ways.

We may not walk on water or find the means to pay our taxes in the mouth of a fish, but from its earliest days, the Church duplicated much of what Jesus did while He was on earth. The authority with which He taught, the trust He had in the Father's will, how He demonstrated the Father's love, the faith He generated in his followers, the power He had over the forces of evil — are all integral to the modeling mission to which we have been called.

Heaven's response to the ungodliness of our generation is found in the lives of men and women just like you and me. The same Jesus who ministered in Galilee is anxious to reveal Himself in our day as well. We must never allow our struggles with faith and the limitations of our human nature negate our call to arms. God has empowered and equipped us with everything we need that we might be effective in modeling the life of the Master.

The Making of a Model

Some years ago, I visited the Dome of the Rock on Jerusalem's Temple Mount, one of Islam's holiest sites. It did not occur to me at the time that I was within perhaps 100 feet of where God Himself had come down in magnificent glory during the time of King Solomon (1 Kings 8).

The evidence of His presence, however, dramatic and unmistakable at the time of the Temple's dedication, had long since vanished by the time Jesus made His historic visit. But God had not abandoned His people. He was back, in the Person of Jesus Christ!

Jesus, a man in *every sense of the word*, was the eternal Son of God. His ministry was without parallel, a majestic and supernatural exercise worthy of His deity. That fact, however, does not deny us the privilege of following in his steps. As the divine Son of God there were aspects of His life that were unique to His mission on earth. As a man, however, His character and personality demonstrated the kind of man every man would have been had it not been for the advent of sin. He was the Prototype, the Perfect Model of what God created us to be.

– Strategies for Living #2 –
No Room at the Inn

There was no room at the Bethlehem Inn that first Christmas eve, not even for a young lady in labor. No one seemed concerned about a pregnant teenager looking for a room in which to deliver her firstborn. It was party time! Nary a gentleman stepped forward, willing to sacrifice the use of his room for the evening. The young couple, consigned to the dark and drafty stable, would have to fend for themselves.

As a matter of fact, this Christmas eve wasn't holiday time for those at the Inn. It would be years before this evening would be celebrated. For the majority, it was just another evening and, in the manger below, just another birth. Few of them would ever know that what took place that night was the greatest event in human history.

It is difficult to describe the uniqueness of that evening. Cleaning up the new baby and preparing Him for His first meal, not even Mary and Joseph realized the impact this night would have on all humanity. As Mary looked her firstborn in the face, little did she know she was looking at the face of God.

It is significant that the first ones to learn of the events of that evening were shepherds. These were hard-working, salt-of-the-earth men, despised commoners, too poor and too busy to enjoy an evening at the Inn. But a host of singing angels had already put them on notice. Something special had taken place; this was one trip to town they would never forget.

They no doubt expected to be welcomed with pomp and ceremony. The heavens had announced the birth of royalty. What they found, however, was lowing cattle, perhaps a donkey or two, and a simple manger scene. For all the hoopla, they were surely surprised to find an apparently normal, newborn baby boy. But looks were deceiving for this precious youngster, although human in the fullest sense of the word, was far from typical. He was God.

Not, I would note, like Adonis, the god of Greek mythology. He was no legend or the product of superstitious belief. This One came out of eternity. He had been there when the world was brought into being. He had walked with Adam, talked with Moses, and joined the three Hebrew children in Nebuchadnezzar's fiery furnace. God Himself had joined the human family.

For those at the Inn, the party would soon be over, but for the shepherds, it was the dawning of a new day. Their hum-drum existence had been crowned with new meaning. They were the first to have an encounter with the living Jesus, and they went home "praising God."

– 4 –

The King Returns to Zion
The Meaning of Jesus' First Advent

Rejoice greatly, Daughter of Zion! Shout, Daughter of Jerusalem! See, your king comes to you, righteous and having salvation, gentle and riding on a donkey, on a colt, the foal of a donkey.

Zechariah 9:9

THE KING WAS BACK! For four hundred years there had been no prophet in Israel. God was there but He had gone silent. And then from out of the wilderness there was heard the voice of one crying, "Prepare the way for the Lord, make straight paths for him. Every valley shall be filled in, every mountain and hill made low, the crooked roads shall become straight, the rough ways smooth. And all mankind will see God's salvation" (Luke 3:4-6).

The Making of a Model

As John the Baptist was fulfilling his calling at the Jordan river, he was approached by a young man in peasant dress. Unannounced, unrecognized, and without fanfare, it no doubt took John by surprise, but the Messiah had arrived.

He looked so ordinary, but this was a different kind of man and heaven could no longer remain silent. Proceedings were suddenly interrupted by the sound of a strange voice. "You are my Son, whom I love; with you I am well pleased" (Mark 1:11). The Baptist could but remark, "Look, the Lamb of God, who takes away the sin of the world!" (John 1:29).

There were healings, there were miracles, and the voice of God was heard again. "Love your enemies ... take up your cross ... your sins are forgiven ... come unto me all of you who are weary and burdened and I will give you rest." This was not the expected message; something new was happening. Not even the prophets understood what was about to take place. But God, in the person of Jesus Christ, had returned to His people.

The Person and ministry of Jesus have been my passion for the last fifty-five years. Although I will never fully understand God, what I can know is disclosed in Jesus. He captured my heart during the days of my youth and I have spent much of my life driven by a passion to understand Him and share my discoveries with my generation.

We must understand the model God has given us to emulate. That role was first given to Adam; he was to set the example for the rest of the human family. But sin destroyed the pattern, and Adam and Eve lost the majesty with which they were created. God, then, gave us a new model. Jesus was the prototype, the Perfect One ... the person each of us was created to be.

Two thousand years have elapsed since those days when God Himself, in the Person of Jesus Christ, was present on earth, speaking in terms we could understand. But despite full access to the record of His life and ministry, Jesus is still largely unrecognized and ignored. If He is to be known, it will be through men and women like you and me, living models of this outstanding Man.

That is an awesome responsibility. If we are to represent Him, if we are to be Jesus to our generation, we must know Him and honor Him in the practical, every-day affairs of our lives. Our society needs to see that our faith in Christ works no matter what the circumstances. Jesus is Lord, and He is meant to be Lord in every area of our lives. In the words of the Apostle Paul,

> Whatever was to my profit, I now consider loss for the sake of Christ. What is more, I consider everything a loss compared to the surpassing greatness of knowing Christ Jesus my Lord, for whose sake I have lost all things. I consider them rubbish, that I may gain Christ and be found in Him. ... I want to know Christ and the power of his resurrection and the fellowship of sharing in his sufferings, becoming like him in his death, and so, somehow, to attain to the resurrection from the dead (Phil. 3:7-11).

In Jesus, I find the perfect model of what God has commissioned us to be.

The love and respect He had for His Father, His sensitivity to human need, and His readiness to challenge the forces of evil were without parallel. He was a man of impeccable character, esteemed and admired by those who knew Him best. Jesus was the prototype, the Master Model, the man every man could have been had it not been for the advent of sin.

I am not sure I am up to the challenge, but I have been captured by this one great objective: to become a living model of Jesus, the Son of God. He was the man I want to be.

I. The I AM and Jesus

I imagine it was early morning when Simeon approached the temple on the forty-first day of Jesus' life (Lev. 12:1-4). The unusual quiet and a slight chill in the air was of little consequence as he made his way through Jerusalem. Simeon was on a mission.

The Holy Spirit had spoken to him; Simeon was soon to meet "the Lord's Christ" (Luke 2:26). As he entered the Temple grounds, he noticed a young couple and their baby boy standing off to one side. They were waiting to celebrate the mother's purification ceremony and the consecration of their first-born son.

Somehow, Simeon knew. *There* was the one he had been looking for. The day, foreseen by the Prophets centuries before, had finally arrived. This baby was to be "a light for revelation to the Gentiles and for glory to your people Israel" (Luke 2:32). Simeon approached the couple and they gave him the privilege of holding their little boy. And he prayed,

"My eyes have seen your salvation, which you have prepared in the sight of all people" (Luke 2:30-31). What an honor it must have been to look into the eyes of Mary's young son, for Simeon was looking at the face of God.

Jesus was truly God and truly man, and He initiated for us the union of heaven and earth. Jesus' first advent was not just to provide the means, and tell us how to get to heaven; He meant to bring heaven down to earth. "Anyone who has seen me," Jesus said, "has seen the Father" (John 14:9).

This was not, however, the first time the Son of God had appeared on earth, in person. Jesus' incarnation marked a new phase in God's relationship with His people but, although unknown to them, He had been there all along.

He was present when, out of a formless void, a habitable world was created. He was in the Garden of Eden in fellowship with Adam and Eve. He had been with Noah, guiding him through the deteriorating state of society's ungodliness and to a new beginning following the great flood. He had eaten lunch with Abraham, appeared to Isaac at Beersheba, and wrestled with Jacob at Peniel.

And then, when the time was right, He appeared to Moses and disclosed the name by which He was to be known. God said to Moses,

> I AM who I AM. This is what you are to say to the Israelites, "The LORD, the God of your fathers—the God of Abraham, the God of Isaac and the God of Jacob—has sent me to you." This is my name forever, the name by which I am to be remembered from generation to generation (Exod. 3:14-15).

The Making of a Model

YHWH, known as Jehovah throughout much of our First Testament, was about to set out on a new journey with His people. There is continuity between the work of God with and through His people Israel and the mission for which Jesus came into our world. YHWH was his name in the First Testament and Jesus Christ in the New. YHWH and Jesus are one and the same.

In the words of Robert Bowman Jr., writing in *Putting Jesus in His Place*,

> Through him all things were made; without him nothing was made that has been made. ... He was in the world, and though the world was made through him, the world did not recognize him (John 1:3, 10).

> Assuming these statements cohere with the Jewish doctrine that YHWH, the Lord God, is the sole creator and maker of all things, the clear implication is that Jesus Christ, the Son, is himself the Lord God (*Jesus Made it All*, paras. 6-7).

Jesus himself verified this in one of His disputes with the Jews. Well aware of the firestorm He was creating, He nevertheless declared openly, *"I tell you the truth, ... before Abraham was born, I am"* (John 8:58).

Repeatedly, Jesus made the claims,
- I am the bread of life;
- I am the light of the world;
- I am the door;
- I am the good shepherd;
- I am the resurrection and the life;
- I am the way, the truth, and the life; and,
- I am the true vine.

From the beginning, the visible form of God was the pre-incarnate second person of the Trinity, identified to Moses as YHWH. Jesus Christ was, and continues to be, heaven's spokesman, God's point of contact with His creation. Besides being the promised Messiah in fulfillment of all the First Testament says about Him, the New Testament pictures him as our advocate (1 John 2:1), our mediator (1 Tim. 2:5), and our "merciful and faithful high priest" (Heb. 2:17).

II. The Return of Israel's King

Following His baptism and forty days in the wilderness, Jesus "began to preach, 'Repent, for the kingdom of heaven is at hand'" (Matt. 4:17). Jesus was letting His people know that now, at last, YHWH was returning to Zion. As if to prove the fact, Matthew goes on to say, "Jesus went throughout Galilee, teaching in their synagogues, preaching the good news of the kingdom, and healing every disease and sickness among the people" (Matt. 4:23).

The Baptist was gone from the wilderness and a new voice was heard. In the synagogues, and on city streets, and in the countryside, people heard a message of hope. "If any man is thirsty, let him come to me and drink. Whoever believes in me, as the Scripture has said, streams of living water will flow from within him." (John. 7:38) And again, "Come to me all you who are wearied and burdened, and I will give you rest." (Matt. 11:28) Jesus was the leader and focal point of the true, returning-from-exile Israel. He was the king through whose work YHWH was, at last, restoring his people.

The Making of a Model

Jesus would soon find His way to Jerusalem to celebrate Passover, but it was not a happy occasion. As He entered the temple, He was incensed to discover that money changers and other commercial interests had desecrated the hallowed grounds.

Few realized what an epic moment this was.

At one time there had been a strategic location, a place of encounter between God and His people. It was known first in the wilderness as the Tabernacle and later, in Jerusalem, as Solomon's Temple. This temple was destroyed by the Babylonians in 586 BC, then rebuilt in the days of Ezra and Nehemiah by Zerubbabel and dedicated in 515 BC. But the Temple soon became a relic of the past. By the time of Jesus' advent, the voice of God had not been heard in Israel for over four hundred years.

In 19 BC, Herod the Great set out to remodel what was left of Zerubbabel's temple, but on a much grander scale. It wasn't that he wanted to glorify God, but it advanced his political agenda. Although the main part was finished in 4 BC the renovation was not fully completed until AD 63.

Gone were the days when, as at the dedication of Solomon's Temple, "the cloud filled the temple of the LORD. And the priests could not perform their service because of the cloud, for the glory of the LORD filled his temple" (1 Kings. 8:10-11). The "house of prayer," the focal point of God's presence, had now become a place of business.

What happened to Temple worship was unacceptable to Jesus. The "throne-room" of God had become a money changer's dream. And twice Jesus let the temple worshippers know how He felt about that. John records this event in the early days of Jesus' ministry; Matthew places a second encounter toward the end. Tables were overturned, money was scattered, and brandishing a whip out of cords, He drove the businessmen from the temple. "Get these out of here! How dare you turn my Father's house into a market" (John 2:16).

Jesus' action in the Temple was a symbolic claim to Messiahship. For centuries, the people of Israel looked forward to the day when the King would return to Zion. In his opening chapter on "the beginning of the gospel about Jesus Christ, the son of God," Mark introduces John the Baptist by quoting Malachi 3:1. "The Lord you are seeking will come to his temple; the messenger of the covenant, whom you desire, will come."

Jesus' cleansing of the temple marked only the beginning of a process that is yet to be fully realized. In the words of the Apostle Paul,

> Israel has experienced a hardening in part until the full number of the Gentiles has come in. And so all Israel will be saved, as it is written: "The deliverer will come from Zion; he will turn godlessness away from Jacob. And this is my covenant with them when I take away their sins" (Rom. 11:25-27).

Despite Israel's rejection of her Messiah, the rebellion of God's people has never altered the divine plan. Sin may have postponed its implementation, but God promises to see it through to completion.

The Making of a Model

And what God did, or is about to do, for the people of Israel, He has done for me. God's presence has been restored, and Jesus Christ has once again become an active force in my life.

During my lonely years, when I was living on the road as a long-haul truck driver, I was away from friends and family. It gave me a chance to reflect on my faith and re-think the role Jesus Christ was to play in my life. How do you model the Master, and do you want to, when you've lost everyone and everything important to you in life?

During my darkest days, however, there was one truth that stabilized my thinking: I never doubted Jesus' resurrection from the dead. As ironic as it may seem, this was the lynchpin, the point of reference, that helped get me back on track. I never questioned the historical record. Jesus died, was buried, and on Sunday morning, was seen alive and well!

And that, in turn, gave me faith to believe that if I would follow Him in obedience and trust, God would make a way for me to climb out of the valley, fight my way through stormy skies, and make it to the mountain-top once again. As simplistic as this may seem, it all came down to Jesus' resurrection.

The resurrection of our Lord was and remains the conclusive evidence of His divine sonship and the validity of His messianic claims. If Jesus was not truly God, He was either a deluded rabbi, a fraud, or a lunatic; you can't have it any other way. But not to worry; Jesus rose from the dead!

That is the essence of the Gospel message, the foundation principle behind *The Making of a Model*. And it is to the resurrection of Jesus we now turn.

– From My Daily Journal #2 –
Jesus, Only Jesus

The Word became flesh and lived for a while among us, and we have seen his glory, the glory of the one and only Son, who came from the Father, full of grace and truth (John 1:14).

Jon Caldwell, in his book on *Christ and Him Crucified*, makes this observation:

> Jesus Christ is the Word who became flesh, dwelt among us as the only righteous Man who ever lived, the only Servant who ever ministered in perfect humility, the only Jew who ever kept the Law of Moses in utmost purity, the only Prophet who ever spoke the words of heaven in supreme verity, the only Son who ever obeyed His Father in absolute honesty, the only Priest who ever interceded for God's people in loving equity, and the only King who ever walked upon the earth with holy authority (III. ITS PROPOSITION, *Condescension and Incarnation*, Para. 3).

This statement is a reminder again of just how important it is for me to place the concentration of my research, study, and work on the Person of Jesus Christ.

It is so easy to get caught up in sustaining my marriage, reading my books, determining my theology, structuring my schedule, focusing on my writing, and dealing with the daily issues that life inevitably brings my way … that Jesus, in His Person, life and sacrifice, gets put in line as just another one of those *issues* with which I must deal as I develop and mature. But not so! Everything I read, think, study, and do must bring me back to Him. He must be preeminent.

Paul, in Eph. 5:25, writes,

> Husbands, love your wives as Christ loved the Church and gave Himself for her.

Paul is a clear case of what I am thinking. Notice that he can't even speak of marriage without getting back to the Person of Christ! Jesus was central to his entire perspective on life, and inevitably, whatever the subject under discussion, Paul got back to Christ. It is that kind of a love relationship with Him that I want to be the guiding force in my life.

Jesus, I note, is not just another *issue* to be studied. He is front and center to everything important to me. He must be acknowledged as my Savior, welcomed as my Lord, worshipped as my God, hallowed as the object of my devotion, and emulated as the only perfect pattern for my life! Theology is not for debate; theology is to be lived, and that living begins with Jesus Christ. He must be everything to me. My research and living must begin, develop, and end — with Jesus! He is what my life is all about!

– 5 –

Joy Comes in the Morning
On the Resurrection of Jesus Christ

If only for this life we have hope in Christ, we are to be pitied more than all men. But Christ has indeed been raised from the dead.

1 Corinthians 15:19-20

IT WAS EARLY MORNING in the city of Jerusalem. Except for the bleating of sheep and the occasional cry of a hungry baby, the city lay quiet in the dawn's freshness. The day gave no hint to the tumultuous events that had taken place just two days before.

Not everyone awakened to the new week with the dread and hopelessness that overwhelmed the followers of the crucified Jesus. For some, the pressure was off. The hated Rabbi was dead; it was time to celebrate.

The Making of a Model

For Pilate and King Herod, a threat to the political stability of their realm was no longer a problem. For Caiaphas and the Chief Priests, the Romans had eliminated a disturbing threat to their authority. For the Pharisees, the Rabbi who had challenged their self-serving hypocrisy was dead. And for the soldiers, a relaxing morning. There would be no insurrection. Finally! Peace and quiet!

But for the followers of the crucified one, the Sabbath marked the end of a terrible week.

For Mary, gone was her firstborn, the one of whom Zachariah had prophesied would be called "a prophet of the Most High … to give His people knowledge of salvation through the forgiveness of their sins" (Luke 1:76-77). For the disciples, an unbelievable disaster as the Romans crucified the finest gentleman they had ever known. For the women, gone was the man who had treated them with dignity and respect. And, for the thousands who had dreamed of a renewed Israel, indescribable disappointment. The Messiah, the One on whom all had pinned their hopes and aspirations, was dead!

And then came Sunday morning.

Just as dawn was breaking, three women made their way to Jesus' tomb. Bringing spices with which to anoint His body, they gave little thought as to how they were going to access the tomb. It was sealed with "a great stone." But they had loved this man as they had no other, and they were determined. They would deal with the details when they got there.

The women had been there Friday evening when Joseph of Arimathea brought Jesus' body for burial to his own new tomb, so they knew where they were going. Since they were not allowed to be on private property, they approached the garden quietly. But when they got there they were surprised to find the soldiers gone and the tomb open; someone had rolled the stone back.

As they prepared to enter the tomb, they did not see two men sitting to the right, just inside the opening. They knew they were at the right tomb; to find it empty was unbelievable. Jesus' body was gone.

Once inside the tomb, they noticed the men. As the men stood, the women bowed, with their faces to the ground (Luke 24:5), overwhelmed. None of this made any sense.

And then, one man spoke. To paraphrase in my own words, I imagine the angel saying, "You looking for someone? If it's Jesus of Nazareth you're looking for, the One who was crucified, He's not here. Come on; don't be afraid. Check it out. Do you see the place where He lay? He's not here; He has risen just as He predicted. Go now! Tell the disciples — and Peter — He plans to meet you shortly in Galilee (Mark 16:2-8).

With scarcely a moment's hesitation, the women ran to inform the disciples. Peter and John, not trusting a woman's word, came charging back to the tomb. And the women were right. There were no soldiers and no body; the tomb was empty!

The record does not tell us what happened to the other two women, but Mary Magdalene left the group and returned to the tomb alone. She couldn't believe the One who had impacted her life so dramatically was gone. Delivered as she had been of "seven devils" (Luke 8:2) and desperate to understand this new turn of events, she couldn't stay away.

As she once again approached the tomb, crying her eyes out, she stooped to look into the tomb and was suddenly aware that there were two angels in the tomb. "Why are you crying," they asked? Perhaps just a bit exasperated, she replied, "Why? They have taken my Lord!"

As she prepared to leave the garden, although it was difficult to see through tear-swollen eyes, she saw someone she presumed to be the caretaker. "If you have carried him away, tell me where you have put him, and I will get him" (John 20:15). It is telling that, so far as we know, the one Mary believed to be the gardener was the only person ever questioned in search of Jesus' body.

As she was turning, the gentleman spoke but one word. Tenderly, in almost a whisper, He said, "Mary!"

For the Magdalene, time stopped. She froze. This could not be. She knew that voice. She had heard her name uttered by countless men, but none had ever come across with tenderness like this one. As unbelievable as it seemed, she *knew* it: Jesus was back!

She whirled around (my take again) and got ahold of him before He could step back. She couldn't believe it. Jesus was there, in person. Wow!

Then Jesus said, "Do not hold on to me" (John 20:17). As much as He loved her, Jesus was about to establish a new relationship with His disciples. The comradery and closeness Jesus had enjoyed with His followers during the previous

5 – Joy Comes in the Morning

three years were to be no more. The new reality was to reflect a spiritual relationship, one not based on touch and sight. He was, however, not finished with Mary, and He had something important for this once wayward woman to do. Go "to my brothers and tell them, 'I am going to return to my Father and your Father, to my God and your God'" (John.20:17).

Mary left, but in a very different frame of mind. It is amazing to note how dramatically one encounter with the Master can influence a person's outlook on life. In just a matter of minutes, Mary's world had changed. I can almost hear her singing, "Happy days are here again! Jesus has risen from the dead!"

I won't attempt to cover all the arguments in opposition to, or in favor of, the real death and literal, physical resurrection of Jesus. When all the facts are taken into consideration, when the historical record is evaluated without prejudice, the evidence for Jesus' resurrection is tantamount to proof.

Our call is to be living models of Jesus the King. Such a call, however, is without merit if Jesus had not risen from the dead. "If only for this life we have hope in Christ," wrote the Apostle Paul, "we are to be pitied more than all men. But," he then added, "Christ has indeed been raised from the dead" (1 Cor. 20).

I. The Message of the Resurrection

There are several issues, such as the existence of God, which the Bible does not attempt to prove. The literal death and resurrection of Jesus Christ, however, is not one of them. This is the one truth Scripture has confirmed as conclusively as possible. To those of us who accept the New Testament record, the evidence is irrefutable: the crucified Jesus was, within three days, alive and once again in contact with His followers.

Critical to this point of view is the message that comes from the empty tomb. Let's look at Jesus' tomb from the perspective of the four groups most impacted by it: the disciples, the Jews, the Church, and Saul of Tarsus.

A. For the Disciples: A Living Lord

Although Jesus had forewarned the disciples of His crucifixion and promised His resurrection, the disciples neither understood nor expected it. Three times, in Mark 8, 9, and 10, Jesus had been clear.

> We are going up to Jerusalem," He said, "and the Son of Man will be betrayed to the chief priests and teachers of the law. They will condemn him to death and will hand him to the Gentiles, who will mock him and spit on him, flog him and kill him. Three days later he will arise" (Mark 10:33-34).

The resurrection was as inconceivable to Jesus' disciples as it is for many today. The Greeks and the Sadducees did not believe in the resurrection, orthodox Jews thought of the resurrection as a future event, and everyone doubted. The men doubted the women (Luke 24:1-12), the disciples doubted Jesus (Luke 24:36-43), and Thomas doubted everyone (John 20:19-25).

The disciples had just spent three years following the Man they believed was the promised Messiah. They had watched as the King returned to Zion. They were there when he fed the

5 – Joy Comes in the Morning

hungry and raised the dead. And then they witnessed Him rejected, tortured, and crucified. And now, so far as they knew, the King was dead!

But early Sunday morning, three women and two gentlemen, distressed beyond belief that Jesus had been crucified, returned to the tomb. To their surprise, the soldiers, following an earthquake that left them terrified, had departed the premises. Miraculously, the tomb was open. And Jesus' body was gone!

But they did not question the authorities, nor did they search for His body. We see them confused and disoriented, afraid that what seemed to have happened was just too good to be true.

Within a matter of days, however, there was a dramatic change of attitude. Mourning gave way to joy, despair gave way to hope, and doubt gave way to faith. And they told everyone who would listen, sometimes at the peril of their own safety, JESUS WAS ALIVE!

B. For the Jews: An Empty Tomb

Skeptics would like you to believe that Joseph of Arimathea had earlier that night moved the body. Perhaps he had the guards drugged, or so the argument goes, and while they slept, he quietly removed Jesus' body from the tomb. But careful consideration of the record demonstrates that this is an argument without substance.

Luke 24:12 relates that Peter, "got up and ran to the tomb. Bending over, he saw the strips of linen lying by themselves, and he went away, wondering to himself what had

The Making of a Model

happened." Luke had no reason to include this detail except that it must have been true: Jesus' body exhumed through the burial wrappings as He rose from the dead, leaving them behind, in place. Only the most gullible would buy the argument that Joseph took time to unwrap the body and leave His wrappings laying in the tomb.

It is inconceivable to think Joseph could have kept such a radical move from the disciples, especially since "the women followed Joseph and saw the tomb and how his body was laid in it" (Luke 23:55). The record is clear: Jesus' closest followers knew nothing about an "Arimathean abduction." Many of them, in fact, later gave their lives defending the reality of Jesus' resurrection.

And how, may I ask, could Joseph have pulled this off? It was Passover weekend, and there were thousands of visitors in town for the celebration. Removing the stone and transporting the body in the dark would have been impossible to do without detection.

And then there is this. The authorities never called either Joseph of Arimathea or the disciples in for questioning. It is apparent that neither Pilate nor the religious community ever doubted the report given by Jesus' followers.

> Matthew argues that the guards were present to prevent any effort to steal the body. There is no other good explanation for why the guards would be present. Nor is it clear, given that no body was ever produced, why Matthew would make up this detail to prevent a "stolen body" theory from arising. It is highly unlikely that the disciples would die for a dead, unrisen messiah whose body they knew had been taken,

much less preach him as risen when they knew otherwise (Bock, *Jesus According to Scripture*, 394).

Everyone knew something extraordinary had taken place. But rather than deal with reality, they washed their hands of the matter. The chief priests met with the elders and devised a plan. They gave the soldiers a large sum of money, telling them, "You are to say, 'His disciples came during the night and stole him away while we were asleep' If this report gets to the governor, we will satisfy him and keep you out of trouble" (Matt. 28:12-14).

If there had been any doubt, the authorities would have done everything in their power to find the body. Producing Jesus' corpse would have doomed the Christian faith. But *they made no such search*. They *knew* that Jesus had risen from the dead.

And, finally, I note this tomb was never venerated as is the custom with the tombs of other important men. In the words of Frank Morrison,

> There is something far more arresting and significant than even this unanimous literary witness ... the extraordinary silence of antiquity concerning the later history of the grave of Jesus. It is strange—this absolutely unbroken silence concerning a spot that must have been a very sacred place to thousands of people outside the circle of the Christian believers themselves. ... Yet we can search in vain for any sign or hint or whisper that during those first four crucial years when the Christians were teaching their strange doctrine within the walls of Jerusalem, there was a stream of pilgrims to that silent grotto beyond the gate (Morison, *Who Moved the Stone?* 90).

The point to all this is that the tomb was empty. Alternate theories, developed by those predisposed to reject the resurrection, demand more faith than accepting the truth. However one restructures the circumstances, the argument that best fits the facts is this: The tomb was empty; Jesus had risen from the dead!

C. For the Church: A New Message

There is a pause that sets in following that first Easter Sunday.

For the next forty days, Jesus' followers disappear. Except for their encounters with the resurrected Messiah, the only thing we hear from them is, "I'm going fishing" (John 21:3). They were facing a new reality. Bewildered and leaderless, all they could do was hold steady and wait until the Master gave them a new set of instructions.

Unaware as they were that Jesus' ascension and the advent of the Holy Spirit were just weeks away, the disciples were utterly disoriented. Jesus had risen from the dead and had met with them, but they had no clue how they would fit into the divine plan. Except for the Apostle John, all of them had abandoned Him when He needed their support the most.

But the days were not wasted. The disciples needed time … time to forgive and be forgiven … time to reorient their thinking to the new reality …time to believe again that God had all things under control.

It is little wonder that the disciples were confused. Two men of God, Jesus and John the Baptist, had proclaimed a message of deliverance, and the Roman authorities had executed them both. "Repent: for the kingdom of heaven is at hand" (Matt. 4:17) now seemed like just so many empty words.

In those remarkable days when Jesus was present to feed the thousands, raise the dead, and teach with authority, they had been looking for the overthrow of the pagan empire. But it had not happened, and, as far as they knew, their most cherished dreams were destroyed on a hill called Calvary.

But things were not as they seemed, and Jesus had not abandoned them. He met with one or more of them on seven different occasions, reassuring them of His love and letting them know He still had a place for them in His Kingdom.

Within fifty days, a new message emerged. God had put the forces of hell in their place, and the Kingdom had come. With the advent of Pentecost, they would soon learn the living Jesus would be with them still. In Jesus' words, "Go and make disciples... Surely I will be with you always, to the very end of the age" (Matt. 28:19, 20).

When Jesus emerged from the tomb, triumphant and majestic, it marked a new beginning, the birth of the Kingdom, the first day of the new creation. This Kingdom would not be found in the precincts of Herod's temple but in the lives of men and women, themselves the temple of the Holy Spirit.

D. For Saul of Tarsus: A New Lord

God's people were given a new message, conclusively proven and beyond question: Jesus had risen from the dead! And yet, unbelievably, some refuse to be convinced. I submit,

The Making of a Model

then, for anyone willing to evaluate the record honestly, one final argument.

Second only to the empty tomb, the strongest evidence we have for the resurrection of our Lord comes from the pen of one of the world's most dedicated unbelievers: Saul of Tarsus.

Far from being an agnostic, the man, later known as the Apostle Paul, was a devoted believer, a sincere and dedicated follower of Jehovah God. He was, in his own words, "a Hebrew of the Hebrews, in regard to the law, a Pharisee, as for zeal, persecuting the church; as for legalistic righteousness, faultless" (Phil. 3:5-6). He was zealous for his God, prepared to defend the divine mandate God Himself had given at Mt. Sinai. There was no way Saul would allow this new faith—which gave the law and everything he believed a new perspective—to go unchallenged.

He was contemporary with Jesus and had perhaps (though he does not say so) seen Jesus during his childhood. We know he was present, as a young man, at the stoning of Stephen in AD 36 or 37, just three or four years after Jesus' death and resurrection.

Stephen's martyrdom had a profound effect on the thinking of this zealous, self-righteous Pharisee. But it would be some years, after doing everything he could to destroy the influence of what he believed to be a fraudulent faith, before things came to a head. And then, on the road to Damascus, he had an encounter with Jesus Himself. And that changed everything.

5 – Joy Comes in the Morning

Saul suddenly realized the reports about the death and resurrection of Jesus were confirmed. He interviewed eyewitnesses and talked with Jesus' brother, James. He may have visited the empty tomb. The evidence challenged everything he believed. And Saul was too honest to deny the truth. After surveying all the facts and interviewing those closest to the action, he concluded ... and spent the rest of his life advocating ... the foundational truth of the Christian faith.

> Christ died for our sins according to the Scriptures, that he was buried, and that he rose again the third day according to the scriptures: And that he was seen of Cephas, then of the twelve: After that, he was seen of above five hundred brethren at once. ... After that, he was seen of James, then of all the apostles. And last of all he was seen of me also, as of one born out of due time (1 Cor. 15:3-8).

Later, in his letter to the Romans, he wrote of Christ Jesus as the "Son, who as to his human nature was a descendant of David, and who through the Spirit of holiness was declared with power to be the Son of God by his resurrection from the dead: Jesus Christ our Lord" (Rom. 1:3-4).

Despite my respect for the many arguments that have been offered in defense of the resurrection, the judgment of Saul of Tarsus is the one that impresses me the most. He was a scholar, a student of the Scriptures, a man of integrity. And he gave the rest of his life in defense of this one, great truth: Thank God Almighty! Jesus rose from the dead!

II. The Story of Burning Hearts

On the afternoon of Jesus' resurrection day, He met with two men, sincere but disheartened disciples, on their way home to Emmaus. Like many of their contemporaries, these two were undoubtedly convinced God would again renew His covenant relationship with the people of Israel. But much of what Jesus had preached and promised now seemed an empty dream; their faith had just been dashed on a cross.

It is significant that, as in the case of Saul of Tarsus, all it took to transform their thinking was one encounter with the living Christ.

> They were talking with each other about everything that had happened. As they talked and discussed these things with each other, Jesus himself came up and walked along with them but they were kept from recognizing him. He said to them, "How foolish you are, and how slow of heart to believe all that the prophets have spoken!" And beginning with Moses and all the prophets, Jesus explained to them what was said in all the Scriptures concerning himself (Luke 24:14-16, 25, 27).

After Jesus explained the divine plan in terms they could understand, He sat down with these two gentlemen for a never-to-be-forgotten supper. What an honor it would have been had you and I been privileged to sit in on *that* conversation. But then, suddenly, "their eyes were opened and they recognized him, and he disappeared from their sight" (Luke 24:31).

It was difficult for them, as it is for many today, to put the death of Jesus in its proper frame of reference. So far from being a defeat, however, it was His high moment of glory. It was indeed a nine-hour nightmare, but it fulfilled the purpose for which He had come to earth, for it doomed the forces of hell and insured our eternal relationship with God.

> Their slowness of heart and lack of belief in the prophets had not therefore been a purely spiritual blindness. It had been a matter of telling and living the wrong story. But now, suddenly with the right story in their heads and hearts, a new possibility, huge, astonishing, and breathtaking, started to emerge before them. ... Suppose the cross was not one more example of the triumph of paganism over God's people but was actually God's means of defeating evil once and for all (Wright, *The Challenge of Jesus,* 162).

What a difference three days can make! From the depths of despair and unbelievable disappointment, the disciple's dreams and hopes found new life in the presence of the living Lord.

Now, finally, the two worlds in which they had been living had come together. Jews and Gentiles, law and grace, the *here and now,* and the *then and there* had all coalesced in the Person of Jesus. The Kingdom He had come to establish was in motion, and they would have a part in spreading the message:

Thank God, Almighty! Jesus has risen from the dead!

His mission accomplished, the King returned to glory. But He had a commission for the motley group of men who had spent quality time with Him. His mission was now to become their mission: "Go into all the world," He told them, "and make disciples" (Matt. 28:19).

The Making of a Model

God had not abandoned His people. It was a new day in the work of God on earth, and now, finally, millions of men and women like you and me would be so dramatically transformed *they* would serve as living models of the Master Himself!

Little did the world realize, indeed, little did *they* know, they were about to launch the movement that would change the course of history.

– From My Daily Journal #3 –
Doing the Work of Believing in Jesus

Then they [the disciples] asked him, "What must we do to do the works God requires?" Jesus answered, "The work of God is this: to believe in the one he has sent." John 6:28-29

In my struggle to determine what I should be *doing* in fulfillment of the call God has placed on my life, this interesting response to a similar question originating with the disciples comes to my attention.

They had followed Jesus, observed the miraculous dimension of His ministry, learned from His teaching, and now seek to determine what this means to: what are they to *do*? And Jesus gives them but one objective: "believe in the one he has sent!"

To believe Him obviously means, first, to take Him at His word. He would, in due time, place before them some monumental challenges. He would ask of them the unreserved commitment of their lives, grant them opportunity to be His representatives to their generation, and that without any promise of immediate reward or release from the pressures of life. All but John would eventually be martyred. Not a one of them could have imagined what the future held but Jesus knew the Father would see to that so long as they lived by this one motto: believe in the One He has sent!

Which is to say that this also meant, secondly, that they were to trust. In the Kingdom of God, belief and trust seem to most generally go hand in hand. To take up the mantle of responsibility following His resurrection, to be His representatives to their generation, would demand a trust that would be developed one experience at a time.

At first glance, Jesus' response seems too simplistic. Like the disciples, I am so caught up in doing ... in the activity of the Kingdom ... that to simply believe Him to lead me one day, one step at a time, just doesn't seem to cut it. Surely there is more to serving God than that! But, at least in this context, that is what Jesus says: believe in Me! Trust me! Walk with Me!

If, indeed, God is far more interested in my growth and maturity than my productivity, then this is clearly my point of departure. There was, obviously, much more to the lives of the disciples than simply believe ... that belief would lead them to change the course of history. But they didn't know that then ... and they weren't ready to accept that dimension of a challenge. But this they could do: they could believe!

And that, I believe, is where God has me! The future is so obscure, the opportunities so limited, the disorientation so pervasive, that I wander in circles wondering where and how to proceed. And then, out of the darkness, comes this word: believe in Me! Trust Me!

He is far more interested in my growth and development than in my activity. He wants me to learn to follow Him, implicitly, without reserve, wholeheartedly. I have prayed for Christlikeness for a lifetime ... and now it is time to trust and wait on God.

PART THREE

Modeling Principles

*Life is not a problem to be solved
but a work to be made.*

~ Philip Yancey ~

– 6 –

Modeling the Master Part I
Modeling Jesus Christ—Your Way

And we know that in all things God works for the good of those who love him, who have been called according to his purpose. For those God foreknew he also predestined to be conformed to the likeness of his Son.

Romans 8:28-29

IT WAS EARLY EVENING in Spokane, Washington, February 1939. As my father stepped into the nursery, he found I had fallen asleep. I was his firstborn, only a few days old, with all the potential inherent in every new life. There lay eight and a half pounds of possibility, created in the image of God.

As I now obviously reconstruct the event, my dad gently placed his hands on my crib and prayed for me.

> Heavenly Father, I cannot tell you how grateful I am for the precious new life that you have placed in our care. I don't know that I'm up to the responsibility, but I thank you for him and promise to do everything within my power to see that he grows up to be a man that serves and honors you. And so, Father, I give Larry back to you; I place him in your care. And Father, please grant me the strength and wisdom to set an example he can follow, and may you be glorified. Amen.

As my father prayed, he was overcome, and he wept. He loved me and could only speculate at what life would bring my way. Had he known, he would not have slept that night.

Life has been difficult for me, much of it of my own making. Even though I was committed from my earliest years to honor and serve the Lord, I ignored the steadying hand my wife could have given to our journey. I withdrew from active ministry at the height of my career, and as a result, spent fourteen years on the road as a long-haul trucker virtually abandoned by my friends and family. But although He was unseen and for some years unrecognized, God was watching over me, gently monitoring my progress.

God never abandoned me. Although there were few life-changing moments or dramatic reminders of His presence during my wilderness years, several events fell into place at just the right time and in just the right way that gave evidence of divine intervention. Remarriage to the sweetheart of my youth, retirement to a home of our own, and emerging from it all debt-free tell only a part of the story.

God has, it seems, honored my father's prayer, monitoring my progress and helping me toward becoming the man I am today. Slowly, but most definitely, I am being reshaped into the image of Jesus Christ.

We are each privileged to have a unique sphere of influence in God's Kingdom. God has men and women strategically placed as living models of His transforming power in every life situation. God's call is universal, but implementing that call is unique to each of us, tailor-made to our station in life, our personality, and the will of God.

I do not know what it is to live with an alcoholic father, to have survived bankruptcy, or to be a single parent. That modeling role is given to others. But I *can* model what it is to have quit the ministry at the height of my career, to have suffered through a senseless divorce, and to have squandered twenty years doing nothing that contributed to my life's mission.

But I can also model how one can rise from the mire of shame and disgust, how a man can recapture a purpose for living, and how a has-been preacher can find a new role of service in the Kingdom of God. It is little wonder that I am optimistic about the future and believe that perhaps the best years of my life still lay ahead.

Because we are each unique, with our own history and sphere of influence, we model the Master in areas and ways that can be fulfilled by no one else. In this and the chapter to follow, I would like to highlight four individuals who emerge from the pages of our New Testament to model the Master in ways unique to their station in life.

First of all, I note,

I. Peter: The Brazen Model

Peter, the fisherman who followed in the footsteps of Jesus, was typical of those who worked the sea in his day. Unfortunately, we have no record nor indication that he had any formal education, and it is likely that, with his abrupt, "in your face" style, he would not have done well as a pastor in one of our modern churches. But God used him to change the course of history.

Peter was direct ... straight from the shoulder. Brazen and unapologetic, it was Peter who dared to walk on water (Matt. 14:29), and it was Peter who used his sword at the time of Jesus' arrest to cut off Malchus' right ear (John 18:10). Peter's daring personality was perfect for spearheading the Church's debut, and God used his boldness and plain-spoken style to launch the most significant social and religious movement the world has ever known.

When Jesus first met Peter, he remarked, "Thou art Simon the son of Jona: thou shalt be called Cephas, which is by interpretation, A stone" (John 1:42, KJV). The transition from "thou art" to "thou shalt be" did not come easy. The Peter who moved the crowd on the day of Pentecost was not the Peter he had been just six weeks before.

Peter's transformation has much to say about the tender way Jesus set about restoring him to the ministry to which he had been called. In Luke 22:32, Jesus told Peter, "I have prayed for you, Simon, that your faith may not fail. And when you have turned back, strengthen your brothers."

Jesus never prayed like that for Judas. Why was that? One commentator referred to this statement as evidence that Peter was "one of the elect" and Judas was not. No way! Judas was a mercenary, a self-centered I'll-do-what-is-best-for-me kind of guy who was determined to betray the Master. Peter, on the other hand, had a soft heart and a deep love for his Lord. Peter may have buckled under pressure, but that did not indicate how he felt about Jesus. Weak and needing to mature, his love for the Master drove him to follow Jesus as best he could through the trial proceedings. Once he was discovered as being one of Jesus' followers, however, "he began to call down curses on himself, and he swore to them, 'I don't know this man you're talking about'" (Mark 14:71) and within minutes "went outside and wept bitterly" (Luke 22:62). It was, perhaps, at that point Peter finally realized something had to change.

Forgotten were the days when Peter dreamed of participating in Israel's revival under the leadership of his Messiah. When challenged, Peter denied even knowing Jesus, and he did so three times over. There was no way Peter could foresee the chance to make amends for his failure, convinced he would never be able to make things right with the Lord of his life. The opportunity to beg Jesus' forgiveness and pledge his loyalty again was out of the question. Jesus, so far as he knew, was dead!

But Peter had not been forgotten. Following Jesus' resurrection, three women appeared at the empty tomb. On entering, they encountered a young man who told them, "Go, tell his disciples *and Peter*, He is going ahead of you into Galilee. There you will find him just as he told you" (Mark 16:7).

Twice Jesus met with the disciples in Galilee. Matthew reported one visit, perhaps the same appearance as the one described by the Apostle Paul in 1 Corinthians 15. A separate incident by the Sea of Galilee is given to us by the Apostle John.

In an encounter that was to prove life-changing for the Apostle Peter, Jesus appeared to the disciples, on this occasion, over a fish and chips breakfast (John 21:11-19). From all appearances, Jesus treated Peter with the same warmth and friendship they had enjoyed for the previous three years.

But Peter was hurting. He was burdened by guilt and desperately needed to recover from a disastrous mistake. Jesus knew that and found an opportunity to address the issue.

> When they had finished eating, Jesus said to Simon Peter, "Simon son of John, do you truly love me more than these?" "Yes, Lord," he said. "You know that I love you." Jesus said, "Feed my lambs." Again Jesus said, "Simon son of John, do you truly love me?" He answered, "Yes, Lord, you know that I love you." Jesus said, "Take care of my sheep." The third time he said to him, "Simon son of John, do you love me?" Peter was hurt because Jesus asked him the third time, "Do you love me?" He said, "Lord, you know all things; you know that I love you." Jesus said, "Feed my sheep (John 21:15-17).

Jesus did not ask if Peter was sorry or whether he had learned from the experience. Jesus did not lecture him, and there was no, "I told you so." Instead, without a single comment about the past, without demanding Peter's commitment, without even granting him the chance to apologize, Jesus asked but one question. "Peter, do you really love me?"

> There are many things going on simultaneously here, but at the center is the challenge to a new way of life, a new forgiveness, a new fruitfulness, a new following of Jesus, which will be wider and more dangerous than what has gone before. ... Peter's change from fisherman to shepherd comes through his facing of his own sin and his receiving of forgiveness (Wright, *Surprised by Hope,* 241)

What Jesus was saying to Peter was that life in God's Kingdom is never defined by one's prior record. Our failures do not determine our future. Peter had been forgiven and recommissioned; he was back on track.

There is a place in the Kingdom of God for those who, like Peter, have a direct, in your face, pull-no-punches style. Following the tumultuous final days in Jesus' life, God needed someone unafraid and ready to face the same crowd that had crucified the Master just days before. Peter was blunt and unrestrained. And effective. In his first message as spokesman for the church, three thousand souls were converted.

One incident, recorded in Acts 3:6, says much about Peter and his stature as a model we can respect. When he encountered a lame man at the Gate Beautiful, Peter said, "Silver or gold I do not have, but what I have I give you. In the name of Jesus Christ of Nazareth, walk" (Acts 3:6).

This Peter was a different Peter from the one who had cowered before a young servant girl's question. His honest self-assessment, his encounter with Jesus, and the transforming power of Pentecost revealed a man never seen before.

And the lame man walked!

II. The Blind Man: The Testimonial Model

The model we now meet is much different from the much-acclaimed Apostle Peter. To society, this gentleman was but another blind man, unheralded and forgotten by his peers. But not so with God.

> As [Jesus] went along, he saw a man blind from birth. ... Having said this, he spit on the ground, made some mud with the saliva, and put it on the man's eyes. "Go," he told him, "wash in the pool of Siloam" (this word means Sent). So the man went and washed, and came home seeing (John 9:1,6).

We have no evidence this man was one of Jesus' followers. And so far as we know, he would have no place in the coming ministry of the church. But God needed another model, and it is instructive He found it in a blind man, an unheralded and nameless beggar. After removing the mud which Jesus had applied to his eyes, the man, for the first time in his life, began to see.

Because his healing took place on a Sabbath, the miracle came to the attention of the Pharisees. Rather than rejoicing with the man, they were incensed. They had little interest in hearing this man's story, and he was in no position to debate the issues. But he had met the Master, and that changed everything.

Had Peter been there, he would have taken the Pharisees to task and read them from the book! James and John might have called fire down from heaven, hoping it would burn them up! Not so the blind man. His message was simple, "One thing I do know, I was blind but now I see!" (John 9:25).

But the Pharisees were not predisposed to buy his story. Their hypocritical attitude and insensitivity toward this man's life-changing experience were telling. Because Jesus did not follow their scruples regarding the law, *they* were the blind ones, unable to acknowledge the remarkable power of Jesus' word. Little wonder Jesus was harsh in his condemnation of these proud, two-faced fanatics. They knew the law, and they knew Jesus but were so narrow-minded and ungodly in their attitude that "Though seeing, they do not see; though hearing, they do not hear or understand" (Matt. 13:13). They looked at the man, and you can feel the harshness of their judgment, "You were steeped in sin at birth," they said, presuming his blindness could have been caused in no other way, and "they threw him out" (John. 9:34).

It has always amazed me to see what just one encounter with Jesus Christ can do to clarify the issues of life. In this man's case, Jesus indicated neither he nor his parents had sinned to cause his blindness, "but this happened so that the work of God might be displayed in his life" (John. 9:3). This day had been planned, in the providence of God, from the day of his birth. His encounter with Jesus was such that when he recognized Jesus as the Son of Man, he could but say, "'Lord, I believe,'" and he worshipped him" (John. 9:38).

> In coming (literally) from darkness to light, he was born again. His story is the case history of a Christian convert. At the beginning he is a beggar and an outcast in the old community of Judaism, and at the end he is a worshiper of Jesus (v. 38) (Michaels, *John,* 160).

It is the story of every Christian. Our society has, tragically, found it surprisingly easy to reject the marvel of transformation we have each experienced. We have a story to tell, but it is significant that "blindness" to the things of God ensures that even a powerful testimony will not be given a fair hearing.

The world may have little interest in what God has done for us and *can* do for them, but we must never hesitate to magnify our God for His transforming power. Every one of us has a story to tell. We may not preach like Peter or write like Paul, but we each have a lifetime of experiences that deserves to be heard. God has been good to us!

We live in a day when truth is relative, God is whomever you want Him to be, and the essence of life is doing as you please. Schemes designed to attract the ungodly and bring them to faith are, except for the miracle-working power of God, carried out with limited success. When there is no interest in Jesus' life and ministry, no sense of sin, and no fear of death, reaching our generation with the claims of the Gospel is almost impossible.

Our testimony is often the only means we have to interest others in the life promised us in Jesus Christ. Critics can question our theology and reject the principles we live by, but they can't deny the change our relationship with Christ has brought to our lives.

Which brings Bob and Betty to mind.

They had been attending our church for some time, and although Betty had already surrendered her life to Christ, it was a tough call for Bob. Surrender to the lordship of Christ, especially when we must acknowledge our sin and the need for forgiveness, is a difficult admission for all of us. For Bob, however, a man who was respected, sophisticated, and very proud, it precipitated a personal crisis.

One night, actually well into the morning hours, his wife was awakened to see Bob sitting up in bed with tears streaming down his face. Suddenly wide awake and startled, she shouted, "Bob, what's wrong?" "Not a thing, Betty. I have just surrendered my life to Jesus Christ!"

The change in his life was immediate. Like the blind man, a sincere response to God's love in Jesus Christ is all it took. From that day forward, Bob was a different man.

Like Bob and Betty, and like you and me, God has a place for every one of us within His Kingdom. Of course, Bob's story would be different than my own, but each of us can witness to the dramatic change Jesus Christ has brought to our lives.

And we are not alone, for God has a place for each of us within His Kingdom. Many serve quietly and in a manner known only to a few, but heaven will honor those who have served in obscurity, lived their lives unheralded, and yet were obedient to the mission God gave them.

Mary Damron, however, is an exception.

As told by Franklin Graham in his book, *Living Beyond the Limits*, Mr. Graham was at home the Friday after Thanksgiving 1994 when he received a call from the receptionist at headquarters. "Mr. Graham, there is a woman out in the parking lot with some shoe boxes for you" (34).

Operation Christmas Child, well-known for sending boxes filled with Christmas gifts to children around the world, was gaining national attention. On entering the lobby, the receptionist pointed him to a little lady that "couldn't have weighed ninety pounds, soaking wet" (F. Graham, 1998, 36). When he introduced himself, the lady from Ikes Fork, West Virginia, came alive.

> "Brother Graham, I'm Mary. Gotcha some shoe boxes fer God. Where do you want them? "
>
> Well, thank you, Mary," he responded. "Why don't you just leave them there in the foyer. We'll stack them up against the wall."
>
> "I gotcha twelve hundred. ... I went up and down the hollers, tellin' everybody that Brother Graham needed shoe boxes fer God" (F. Graham, 1998, 36).

Franklin Graham was impressed.

By Christmas 1995, Mary had her mission in full swing and came in with six thousand boxes; she was rapidly becoming a local celebrity.

After being written up in the local West Virginia newspaper, she caught the attention of the White House.

> "Coal Miner's Wife to Meet President of the United States" read the headlines and accordingly, the day came when Mary stood in the Oval Office chit-chatting with the President of the United States.
>
> The "little lady," however, wasn't quite through. "Mr. Prez-i-dent, I got somethin' fer you," and she handed him a copy of Frank Graham's book, *Miracle in a Shoebox*. And then, reaching into her bag, she took out an empty shoebox. "Mr. Prez-i-dent, will you fill this one fer me?"
>
> And then, "Mr. Prez-i-dent, do you care if I pray fer you?" As per Franklin Graham, "Mary took the lead in joining our hands and then prayed a short prayer. "Our heavenly Father, we pray for the Prez-i-dent and all the responsibilities he has on his shoulder. ... We pray that You would watch o'r him and protect him and give him strength fer this day. In Christ's name we pray. Amen." (F. Graham, 1998, 47-48).

As it happened, the President was planning to send troops to Bosnia to implement the Dayton Peace Accord. It was scheduled to be signed in France within just a few days.

> "Mary, how would you like to go with us to Bosnia and help give these boxes away? ... She was such a blessing. She put her arms around those kids, she prayed with them, she cried with them, she touched them. At times, she even acted like one of them!" (F. Graham, 1998, 38-39).

Who would have ever believed that Mary Damron would make such an impact on so many lives? But isn't that just like God? There is no limit to what He can do when He finds an open and willing heart. He is the God of the impossible, and it is exciting to see that He is still transforming men and women just like you and me into living models of the Master Himself.

– Strategies for Living #3 –
If There Is No God

He was a young man with a future. As the only man left in the family, he was fortunate to have a dedicated mother who took in washing to put her ambitious son through Seminary. She was hoping for a priest; what she got was a monster.

The Tbilisi Georgian Orthodox Seminary was no place for a young Joseph Stalin. Impressed by the writings of Karl Marx, he gave up on God to pursue a career dedicated to social change and personal power. He failed to make the priesthood, but as a self-serving insurrectionist, he was a smashing success.

After Lenin died in 1924, Stalin set out to destroy the old party leadership, executing potential rivals and assuming the position as leader of the Soviet Union. Although he transformed the Soviet state from a peasant society into an industrial and military superpower, he is best remembered for the death of as many as twenty million of his own people, executed to perpetuate his hold on power.

At some point in the process, Joseph Stalin had to face life's most important question: What will you do with God? We have each inevitably had to deal with that question and where we came out, what we decided, was a determining factor in the person we have become.

The Making of a Model

What if there is no God? What if Jesus was a fraud and Christianity a bogus faith?

If there is no God, there is no coherent meaning to life. Without God, you lose the sacred essence of human existence. What meaning do you attach to life? Your presence on earth is an accident, your journey through life, survival of the fittest, and your death, a meaningless end.

And if there is no God, there is no life after death, and this is the only heaven you will ever know; this is as good as it gets! Your dreams and drives end at the grave; there is no tomorrow. And for Joseph Stalin or Mother Teresa, it's all the same.

If there is no God.

But that is the question, isn't it? And God has given us an answer in the life, message, and resurrection of His Son. "Anyone who has seen me," Jesus said, "has seen the Father." Our access to God, what we can know of Him, what our finite minds are capable of understanding, comes through and only through Jesus Christ.

The Apostle John had it right. "In Him was life," he wrote, "and that life was the light of men." If you are to find meaning to your existence, purpose to your journey, and the peace of mind that comes from knowing eternal life awaits, you have only one alternative: Jesus must be the Lord of your life. And what you do with Him is going to make all the difference in your world.

– 7 –

Modeling the Master Part II
Modeling Jesus Christ—Your Way

But whatever was to my profit I now consider loss for the sake of Christ. What is more, I consider everything a loss compared to the surpassing greatness of knowing Christ Jesus my Lord.

Philippians 3:7-8

IN 1 PETER 2:21 WE READ, "To this you were called, because Christ suffered for you, leaving you an example, that you should follow in his steps."

That is our mandate. And Katie Davis is a classic case in point.

Katie was a popular eighteen-year-old, senior class president, and homecoming queen from Nashville, Tennessee. Following a Christmas holiday visit to Uganda in 2006, she accepted an invitation by the director of an

The Making of a Model

orphanage in Uganda to join them as their Kindergarten teacher. On her first morning in class, prepared for a group of fourteen, one hundred and thirty-eight showed up, and Katie's heart was lost to her kids.

Katie left her family, abandoned the comfort and safety of life in central Tennessee, and settled in Uganda. In time she adopted thirteen girls who called her mama. It is a fascinating account, told in her book, *Kisses from Katie*. One incident, which took place after a short break for a one-semester attempt at a college education, tells the story.

> One of my favorite mornings after I returned to Uganda began when my three oldest daughters marched into my room, where I was still sleeping. 'Mommy, there are children we need to help, please.' 'Okay,' I said groggily, 'where?'
>
> They took me to the abandoned house down the road. In the back room were seven children on the dirt floor. They were completely filthy and starving. The oldest was eleven and the youngest was two years old. I had never seen children so sick. ... They all had severe ringworm, malaria, and scabies ... among other conditions. Two of them were the skinniest human beings I had ever seen.
>
> Of course, the girls and I took them home. I have never been so proud of my family as I was when I watched their reaction. Prossy, Margaret, and Agnes went straight to the tub to give the children baths. ... In less than an hour, our seven neighbors were a new bunch of children — bathed, dressed, fed, and giggling. ...
>
> This was one of many, many times I have watched my children embrace and welcome in our home strangers and people in need. ... How beautiful it is to watch the unwanted

feel loved and important, to watch strangers become family members" (*Kisses from Katie*, 141-142).

Katie Davis may seem to be a special case, but at the beginning of her journey, Katie was a typical teenage girl with plans for a college education and, perhaps, marriage to the special man in her life. But she had a love for children, a driving desire to serve, and a willingness to follow in His steps no matter where that led. With each act of obedience, another door opened, and the rest, as they say, is history.

That is Katie's story ... a fascinating opportunity to model the Master in a setting consistent with her personality and station in life. But she is not alone, for each of us is granted the privilege to represent the Master, most generally in a setting and a manner that can be fulfilled by no one else.

It is fascinating to discover what God can do, as in the case of the two individuals that follow, when He finds a willing heart. No matter where we are in life, God has a place for us whereby we, too, can serve as living models of Jesus Christ.

III. Paul: The Intellectual Model

Most of us, at least those of us in some phase of active ministry, are predisposed to concentrate on our calling. We want to serve, take on the forces of evil, make an impact for the Kingdom of God. Our impulse, our drive, is to *do* something for God.

God, however, seems far more concerned about who we *are*. Much of God's work in our lives will best be understood

The Making of a Model

when we realize He is leading us toward becoming effective, living models of Jesus Christ.

> A few years ago a brother came to [Mother Teresa] complaining about a superior whose rules, he felt, were interfering with his ministry. 'My vocation is to work for lepers,' he told Mother Teresa. 'I want to spend myself for the lepers.' She stared at him a moment, then smiled. 'Brother,' she said gently, 'your vocation is not to work for lepers, your vocation is to belong to Jesus,' (Colson, *Loving God*, 126).

No man personified this principle, as did the Apostle Paul. In 1 Cor. 2:2-5, he writes,

> I resolved to know nothing while I was with you except Jesus Christ and him crucified. I came to you in weakness and fear, and with much trembling. My message and my preaching were not with wise and persuasive words, but with a demonstration of the Spirit's power, so that your faith might not rest on men's wisdom, but on God's power.

Nothing happened to transform this brilliant and sincere Jew into the great spokesman for the Christian faith, however, *until he met Jesus* face to face.

Saul of Tarsus, the Osama bin Laden of the early church, was a proud, self-righteous Pharisee. He rejected the Christian message as without merit, believing it to have been founded on falsehood and a perversion of God's truth.

The first we hear of him is in a postscript to Stephen's martyrdom. "And Saul was there, giving approval to his death" (Acts 8:1). We are not told how much of an influence that experience had on his thinking, but the next time we hear of him is in Acts 9:1-4.

> Saul was still breathing out murderous threats against the Lord's disciples. He went to the high priest and asked him for letters to the synagogues in Damascus, so that if he found any who belonged to the Way, whether men or women, he might take them as prisoners to Jerusalem. As he neared Damascus on his journey, suddenly a light from heaven flashed around him. He fell to the ground and heard a voice say to him, "Saul, Saul, why do you persecute me?"

I have always been impressed by the dramatic impact one encounter with Jesus Christ can have on a person's life. For Saul of Tarsus, it was an experience that took but a few minutes, but for him and for the church, it was historic. So complete was his transformation, he made an impact on the Church and the people of his generation that was second only to Jesus Himself.

First of all, I note, he was ...

A. A Man of Remarkable Integrity

The transition from Saul, the devoted and arrogant Jew, to Paul, God's man of the hour, was not an easy one.

Saul had studied under Gamaliel, a highly respected teacher of the Law. He was a "Hebrew of the Hebrews ... a Pharisee; ... touching the righteousness which is in the law, blameless" (Phil. 3:5, 6). He was a good man, anxious to support the directives given to the people of Israel by God Himself. There was, in his view, no way Jesus could be the Messiah. The Law declared that "anyone who is hung on a tree is under God's curse" (Deut. 21:23). Jesus had to be a fraud!

> The conclusive argument was simply that Jesus had been crucified. A crucified Messiah was a contradiction of terms. ... The Messiah, practically by definition, was uniquely endowed with the divine blessing — "the Spirit of the Lord shall rest upon him" (Isa. 1:2) — whereas the divine curse explicitly rested on one who was crucified. When [Saul] was first confronted by people who publicly affirmed that the crucified Jesus was the Messiah, the course was clear: they were guilty of blasphemy, and should be dealt with accordingly" (Bruce, *Paul: Apostle of the Heart Set Free*, 70-71).

But then, on the way to Damascus, it took but a few minutes for the entire course of his life to be changed. Suddenly, "out of the blue," a voice was heard, and it was not, I note, "Saul, Saul, why do you persecute Christians?" It was, and I believe this was significant to him, "Saul, Saul, why do you persecute *me*?"

It was a historic moment, for him and for the church. As unbelievable as he found it to be, he was compelled to acknowledge that Jesus was alive, vindicated, and exalted by God.

If we were to define integrity as strict adherence to a code of moral values, uprightness, and honesty, then Saul, soon known as the Apostle Paul, was all of that. He wasn't persecuting the church because he had a mean streak. He was convinced, with support from the First Testament revelation, that this new religious philosophy was unacceptable to the God he served.

7 – Modeling the Master Part II

Saul's encounter with Jesus on the road to Damascus, however, changed all that.

> Last of all he appeared to me also, as one abnormally born. For I am the least of the apostles and do not even deserve to be called an apostle, because I persecuted the church of God. But by the grace of God, I am what I am (1 Cor. 15:8-10).

And the same dedication he had given to persecuting the church, he now gave to proclaiming its message. Only a man of unqualified integrity could make such a transition. He understood the opposition as few others and was able to challenge them on their own terms. He had, after all, been one of them.

Many sincere Christians, recently converted from Judaism, were convinced the Law of Moses should have a prominent place in the church's life. The Law had been given to Moses by God Himself and had guided the people of Israel for better than fourteen hundred years. But Paul's newfound faith precipitated a fundamental change in his theology. In a dramatic reversal, he now had a new message: salvation was not by the works of the Law, but by grace, through faith.

It was a significant turnaround. The law had been the magnet that pulled together all the elements of his life and thought. It gave purpose and meaning to his faith. When he was finally able to reframe the law in the light of the Gospel, he found a new "model" that would consume him for the next thirty years. His name was Jesus Christ.

Secondly, Paul was ...

B. A Man of Outstanding Dedication

The Apostle's commitment to Jesus Christ can be seen in the significant personal sacrifice he made on behalf of the church.

> Though I am free and belong to no man, I make myself a slave to everyone, to win as many as possible. To the Jews I became like a Jew, to win the Jews. To those under the law I became like one under the law. ... To the weak I became weak, to win the weak. I have become all things to all men so that by all possible means I might save some (1 Cor. 9:19-23).

It was not a formula designed to garner popular support. He alienated many who saw him as hypocritical and misguided. But Paul was man enough to live by his ethical convictions and leave the results to God. It was an attitude he maintained through to the very end of his life, sometimes at great personal cost.

We see this in an incident, recorded in Acts 16:16-40 that took place in Philippi.

While going "to the place of prayer" (vs. 16), we are told he met a demon-possessed slave girl who had been predicting the future and earning good money for her owners. When Paul commanded the spirit to come out of her, she was miraculously delivered. But she lost her money-making capability and her owners were incensed!

The riot that ensued found Paul and Silas arrested, severely flogged, and put in prison. Sometime around midnight, an earthquake shook the city of Philippi. The prison doors came open, the chains came off, and Paul, Silas, and the other prisoners were suddenly free. The jailor was about to kill himself, believing all had escaped. But Paul stopped him and "spoke the word of the Lord" (vs. 32) to him. The upshot of it all was that the jailor and his family were "filled with joy because they had come to believe in God" (vs. 34).

Paul and Silas were released from prison the following day. The magistrates then learned they were Roman citizens, and the authorities knew they were in deep trouble. As Roman citizens, they should never have been flogged or imprisoned.

Then why did they not tell of their Roman citizenship the previous day? It would have saved them from a severe flogging and a night in prison. What prompted Paul to keep it a secret? We are given no clue, but it precipitated an opportunity for ministry that, even at great sacrifice, Paul and Silas could not pass up. And God honored their endeavor; the jailor and his family were converted and "filled with joy" (vs. 34).

Paul and Silas took a beating, but they left a message of personal courage and God's grace that could have been delivered in no other way.

Finally, Paul was ...

C. A Man of Extraordinary Humility

The Apostle was sold out to Jesus Christ.

Once he met the Lord and was convinced of the truth of the Gospel, he was able to say quite honestly to King Agrippa, "I was not disobedient to the vision from heaven" (Acts 26:19). From the moment of his conversion, the Apostle Paul was committed to model the Master. "Follow my example," he

The Making of a Model

wrote to the Corinthian church, "as I follow the example of Christ" (1 Cor. 11:1).

Implications from his writings indicate Paul was not impressive in person and apparently not a great speaker. In 2 Cor. 10:10 he writes, "For some say, 'His letters are weighty and forceful, but in person he is unimpressive and his speaking amounts to nothing.'" But Paul had a brilliant mind and a commitment to live the will of God. It made him second only to Jesus in the influence he had on the theology and ministry of the Church.

There is much about the Apostle Paul that I admire, but perhaps second only to his commitment to Christ, I am impressed by his amazing humility.

A genius of remarkable insight, he was nevertheless honest enough to realize the impact his unique ministry could have on his battle with pride. In 2 Cor. 12:7-10, he wrote,

> To keep me from becoming conceited, because of these surpassingly great revelations, there was given me a thorn in my flesh, a messenger of Satan to torment me. Three times I pleaded with the Lord to take it away from me. But he said to me, "My grace is sufficient for you, for my power is made perfect in weakness." Therefore I will boast all the more gladly about my weaknesses so that Christ's power may rest on me. That is why, for Christ's sake, I delight in weaknesses, in insults, in hardships, in persecutions, in difficulties. For when I am weak, then I am strong.

As Paul matured, note the evolution in the way he thought of himself.

7 – Modeling the Master Part II

- Written around AD 53, Paul wrote to the Corinthians, "For I am *the least* of the apostles and do not even deserve to be called an apostle" (1 Cor. 15:9)
- Written around AD 58, Paul wrote to the Ephesians, "Although I am *less than the least* of all God's people, this grace was given to me" (Eph. 3:8)
- Written around AD 65, Paul wrote to Timothy, "Christ Jesus came into the world to save sinners; of whom *I am chief*" (1 Tim. 1:15).

There is a progression here that speaks to me; I admire his humility.

But I am also impressed by his willingness to suffer in defense of the Gospel.

Paul was as susceptible as any of us to the pleasures of an easy, comfortable life. But he gave it up, accepted the suffering that came with God's call, and did so without complaint.

Serving the Lord was never meant to be a walk in the park. Paul struggled through most of his ministry with a "thorn in the flesh." It was, I am convinced, a severe problem with his eyes, dating back to his conversion. Living with a personal handicap, resisting the opposition to the gospel of grace, a driven man who spent several years in prison, it was a tough life. I applaud his attitude as he writes,

> At my first defense, no one came to my support, but everyone deserted me.... But the Lord stood at my side and gave me strength, so that through me the message might be fully proclaimed and all the Gentiles might hear it. And I was delivered from the lion's mouth. The Lord will rescue

me from every evil attack and will bring me safely to his heavenly kingdom. To him be glory for ever and ever. Amen (2 Tim. 4:16-18).

Perhaps this is of particular importance to me, for I have never done well with my peers in the ministry. I am undoubtedly subject to criticism, and I presume Paul was also, but I admire his attitude toward those who dismissed him as obstructionist and misguided. Paul's peace of mind rested not on his popularity but on God's approval.

It is a model I want to emulate.

IV. Matthew: The Social Model

It is interesting to note that even though all of our models had a similar message, each of them served the Lord in a style all their own.

Shortly after his call to be one of Jesus' disciples, Matthew, known here as Levi, "held a great banquet for Jesus at his house, and a large crowd of tax collectors and others were eating with them" (Luke 5:29). Before he lost touch with the friends with whom he had worked and who knew him well, Matthew wanted them to meet Jesus. The change in his character, the new direction his life had taken, was something he hoped would make an impression on his friends.

Tax collectors were known for their dishonesty. They commonly charged more than the law demanded and kept the over-billing for themselves. But something had happened to Matthew: he had met the Master. He left his lucrative profession and committed his life to follow the Rabbi from Nazareth.

There is no evidence Matthew threw this party at *Jesus'* behest. But Matthew was so overwhelmed by the privilege Jesus had given him he could not leave familiar surroundings without giving his friends an explanation.

And, typically, the Pharisees and teachers of the law were disturbed that Jesus would spend time with such riffraff. To their chagrin, however, Jesus was comfortable visiting with Matthew and his colleagues. We have no evidence Jesus said or did anything, although He presumably carried on a lively conversation with all those around Him. But "the Son of Man has come to save that which was lost" (Matt. 18:11), and He was not about to allow the religious right to prevent Him from associating with a group of people desperately in need of His love and compassion.

It is a lesson we all need to take to heart. So distorted has our society become, sometimes with aberrant lifestyles we find intolerable, it is difficult for us to love others with the same measure of commitment with which God has loved us. But if we wish to model the Master, we *must* deal with our own discomfort and judgmental attitudes and love even the most deviant among us, unconditionally. Calvary love has no limits!

This is the model with which I am most comfortable. I don't have the intellect to debate like the Apostle Paul, or the boldness of a man like Peter, but meeting other men over lunch fits my nature perfectly. Business acquaintances, friends, and people new to the church have joined me for lunch and allowed me to share my personal story and highlight the joy I have found in serving Jesus Christ. The breakfast engagement to which I refer in the Appendix is only one case in point.

Luncheon appointments weren't that difficult to set up, especially with professional people, and during those meals I was able to present Jesus in a setting that was relaxed and enjoyable to us both.

On one occasion the agent for an office supply store that serviced our church met me for lunch. It wasn't too long into our conversation before he remarked with a smile, "I was wondering why you would ask me out for lunch. Now I know!" And for forty-five minutes, over a great lunch, I had a chance to present the claims of the Gospel, perhaps for the first and only time in his life.

It is for each of us a challenge to find a means and opportunity to share our faith. We may not have the intellect of a man like Paul or the public forum given to the Apostle Peter, but we all have a story to tell. Like that blind man, we can tell our family and friends, "One thing I do know. I was blind but now I see!" (John 9:25).

As never before in the history of our great nation, America needs men and women willing to stand and be counted as living models of the Master. Our world needs to see Jesus exemplified in the lives of people just like you and me. Sometimes we model the Master when the sun is shining and we can testify to the great blessing that is ours in knowing the

Lord. And then there are those other times when our modeling is done during moments of darkness and stress.

My point is best illustrated by an incident related by Larry Campolo, writing in *Wake Up America*.

> A moving expression of grace was provided by the parents of a graduate of the college where I teach when their son, a young Korean man, was brutally and senselessly murdered on the streets of Philadelphia. In Ho Ho had graduated with honors from Eastern College and was in the process of completing graduate studies in medicine at the University of Pennsylvania when he was killed. While mailing a letter to his family in Korea, he was surrounded by a gang of teenage hoods, robbed of the change in his pockets, and beaten to death.
>
> Even though there are murders daily in the City of Brotherly Love, the ugliness and callous nature of this murder sent shock waves through the city. The police went all out to find the culprits and within three days had them behind bars.
>
> The murderers proved to be a sorry lot. They were homeless boys who had grown up on the streets, "throw-away" kids not wanted by anyone. They were illiterate and unskilled and had learned to survive in their cold and violent ghetto by becoming cold and violent themselves.
>
> When the trial of these murderers was held, In Ho Ho's parents flew to America to be in attendance. They sat motionless all during the legal proceedings. They said nothing at all during the trial. They only asked for an opportunity to speak after the "guilty" verdict was announced. It was then that they stepped forward and kneeled in front of the judge's bench.
>
> Before a stunned audience, these parents begged for mercy for their son's murderers. Not only were they devoid of any

"an eye for an eye and tooth for a tooth" mentality, but they wanted to help these despicable young men.

They begged the judge to release their son's murderers to them so that they could give the boys the home and care they had never had. They were Christians, they explained to the judge, and they wanted to show something of the grace they had received from God to those who had done them such grievous evil.

The judge, who newspaper reporters claimed had a reputation for being hard and unemotional, had tears in his eyes as he explained, "That is not the way our system of justice works" (47-48).

And *that* is what it means to be ... a living model of Jesus Christ!

–Strategies for Living #4 –
From Useless Refuse ... a Masterpiece

In 1501, a twenty-six-year-old Italian artist was given an unfinished sculpture and commissioned to create a statue of the Biblical hero David for the Cathedral of Florence. To be created from a huge block of granite, it seemed to many an impossible task. But Michelangelo saw something others had missed, and in three years' time, he was able to create a masterpiece that has been hailed by many as the greatest statue created by human hands.

The original commission had been given Agostino di Duccio in 1464. He got as far as shaping the legs, feet and the torso, but abandoned the project in 1466. Ten years later Antonio Rossellino was commissioned to pick up where Duccio had left off, but his commission was soon cancelled.

For the next twenty-five years, this block of marble lay discarded, exposed to the elements in the courtyard of the Opera del Duomo. It was, for some, a useless piece of refuse. But Opera authorities, hoping to resurrect the dead project, commissioned Michelangelo to see if he could breathe life into the inert piece of stone.

The two previous artists had abandoned the project, convinced that imperfections in the stone might threaten the stability of the statue. But Michelangelo looked past the defects and saw what it could be. For the next three years, he chiseled away at

The Making of a Model

the excess, and from the huge piece of granite, there emerged a stunning masterpiece.

The depiction of David, poised and ready for combat, was inherent in the stone all along. It only took the vision and endeavor of a master sculptor to bring it to light. And that is how God sees you and me.

"We are God's masterpiece." writes the Apostle Paul. "He has created us anew in Christ Jesus, so we can do the good things he planned for us long ago."

"Jesus didn't die just to get us off the hook. He also died to resurrect the person we were destined to be before sin distorted the image of God in us. And He doesn't just set us free spiritually. He also sets us free emotionally and relationally and intellectually. We are held captive by so many things … by our imperfections and insecurities … by our guilt and anxiety … by expectations and lies and mistakes. Jesus died to set us free from all the above. … He sets us free to become who we were meant to be" (Mark Batterson, *Soulprint*, 11).

We may be haunted by failure, overwhelmed with guilt, and limited by our mistakes, but in God's kingdom, our deficiencies do not determine our destiny. Our God is a God of second chances. He knows who we are, but He also knows what we can become. The world may see a hardened, marred piece of granite; God sees a masterpiece.

God has a unique plan for your life, a destiny that is different from that of anyone who has ever lived. He wants to take you as you are and where you are, that He might remold you into something you could never be without Him. In the hands of the Master Craftsman, you too can discover there is no limit to what God can do when He finds a willing heart.

– 8 –

Designed for Leadership

How to Respond to America's Moral Crisis

You are the light of the world. ... Let your light shine before others, that they may see your good deeds and glorify your Father in heaven.

Matthew 5:14, 16

DENNIS PRAGER, in an interview aired on the Fox Business Network, April 2, 2018, stated, "This is the first generation in human history ... that is being raised godless. ... and the results, I believe, are the end of Western civilization as we know it."

That may sound extreme, but Dennis Prager is not alone in his opinion. Many of us, startled by the social changes that have taken place in America in just the last ten years, believe America is in deep trouble.

The Making of a Model

We are a nation at war. And it is not being fought with guns and bombs; it's being fought with words and ideas. And it is not just political; this is a generational, social, and religious war being fought in our legislatures, churches, classrooms, and on the streets of our cities. Opposing sides are vying for attention, each of which has a different vision for America.

As was evident during the progressive upheaval in early 2020, militant special interest groups have demanded of both industry and government not just tolerance but approval. Our society has shown a willingness to accept even the most extreme social aberrations in defiance of those issues that have, for centuries, been the hallmark of the Christian faith. Branded as homophobic, racist, and intolerant, Christians now have little voice in determining the future of our great country.

This turn away from God has left its mark on our society. Militants and progressives have always been with us. What is most disturbing, however, is that they have now generated a following and found widespread support.

Abortion by lethal injection—until the day of birth—is now legal in New York State. Gov. Andrew Cuomo, to the sounds of a cheering crowd, signed the "most aggressive women's equality platform in the United States" on Jan. 24, 2019.

A moratorium on execution in the state of New York has been in place since June 2004. Certain crimes that fall under the federal government's jurisdiction are still subject to the death penalty, but death sentences are no longer sought at the state level. It is telling that the state does not allow you to administer a lethal injection to rapists, murderers, and pedophiles, but now permits ending the life of his baby, even until the day of its birth.

David Jeremiah, in his book, *Is This the End,* writes,

> In 2011, I wrote a book titled *I Never Thought I'd See the Day*. ... As I wrote in that book, I never thought I'd see the day when marriage would be obsolete, morality would be in free-fall, and the church would become irrelevant to society.
>
> In the ensuing half-decade since that book, those cracks that riddled America's foundation have spread into gaping fissures, and many more have appeared. Morality in the United States is no longer in free fall; it has hit rock bottom. In today's America, anything goes. Christianity is no longer merely being pushed aside; American Christians are now experiencing overt repression and even persecution (VII).

God has blessed us as a nation. I consider it a privilege to live in these United States, and I'm honored to be the patriarch of a family that is doing well and would make any man proud. But I fear for their future. Our society has demonstrated it has few limits on how far it will go to satisfy selfish interests. America, as a case in point, has vigorously defended the right to gender reassignment and gay marriage, but in a perverted twist of moral responsibility, denied the right to life to the unborn.

So how does one respond to the challenges that lie before us? Some are in denial, scarcely aware of the depth of the moral evil that has gripped our nation. Others have given in to despair, convinced there is little we can do to reverse trends that are rapidly becoming entrenched.

For several years following retirement, I drove a school bus for the Winnisquam School District in Tilton, NH. The forty people I worked with were, so far as I could tell, honorable men and women and a pleasure to be around. Even though I was low-key regarding my faith, they all knew where I stood and respected me accordingly. Ironically, however, not once in the ten years I worked with them did one of them ask a single question regarding the Bible, God, the church, or my point of view. It's not that they were being unkind; they simply had no interest. They were, I believe, typical of what I see happening in America today. It is nearly impossible to influence a society that has little interest in God, no concept of sin, and no apparent fear of death.

But we must not dismiss our fellow Americans to their own fate. God has called us to be "a chosen people, a royal priesthood, a holy nation, a people belonging to God, that [we] may declare the praises of him who called [us] out of darkness into his wonderful light" (1 Pet. 2:9). We *must* take that responsibility seriously.

I. The Divine Mandate

The spiritual state of our society demands that God's people, commissioned to model the Master, do so boldly and without apology. We are to be Jesus to our generation, living models of how He would serve and what He would say to modern America. We are God's representatives, His means of contact with a society desperately in need of change.

A. The Mandate to Administrate

From the very beginning, God meant for the administration of His Kingdom to be in the hands of His people. God's mandate to populate and care for His creation came first in the Garden of Eden. God blessed Adam and Eve and said to them, "Be fruitful and increase in number; fill the earth and subdue it. Rule over the fish in the sea and the birds in the sky and over every living creature that moves on the ground" (Gen. 1:28).

One cannot imagine what life on earth would have been like had Adam and Eve never sinned. Just think! Perfect legislators, directing our political affairs; perfect educators, teaching unbiased truth; perfect drivers, always watching out for the other man; perfect children, always obeying and learning from perfect parents. Unbelievable!

That is what God had in mind and, I am convinced, will, indeed, take place on earth at a time yet to come. God's plan to have His created beings living in a world without evil has been delayed in its implementation, but it has not been destroyed. The Bible promises a thousand-year period when Satan will be bound, and the society God had planned will come into being. What God envisioned for our society will still come to pass, an example to all humanity of what was in the heart of God when He brought man into being.

But that is not how things worked out. Adam and Eve sinned, and the divine plan, which God will most certainly implement at a time yet to come, was put on hold.

> The Lord saw how great man's wickedness on the earth had become, and that every inclination of the thoughts of his heart was only evil all the time. The Lord was grieved that he had made man (Gen. 6:5-6).

This precipitated the great flood by which God destroyed almost all living things. Only Noah and his family survived, and to them, God renewed the mandate.

> Be fruitful and increase in number and fill the earth. ... Everything that lives and moves about will be food for you. Just as I gave you the green plants, I now give you everything (Gen. 9:1,3).

B. The Mandate to Model

Despite our royal commission, the history of the human family is one of repeated failure after failure. God's covenant with Noah, and His subsequent covenant with Abraham, came down to this: for the four hundred years prior to the birth of our Lord, there had been no prophet in Israel. Heaven had gone silent.

And then, "when the time had fully come, God sent his Son, born of a woman, born under the law, to redeem those under law, that we might receive the full rights of sons (Gal. 4:4-5). Finally, a Perfect Model was given to us; finally, we could see the kind of person God had created each of us to be.

> To this you were called, because Christ suffered for you, leaving you an example, that you should follow in his steps (1 Pet. 2:21).

Living models of the Master! What an incredible privilege!

I am well aware of the task that lies before us. We are facing a day of spiritual ignorance beyond anything we could have imagined. It is not, however, our place to curse the darkness; our challenge is to turn on the light.

Perhaps as a sign of the end times, Jesus said, "Because of the increase of wickedness, the love of most will grow cold" (Matt. 24:12). It has been on our watch that our young people have been led to believe there is no such thing as absolute truth, no evidence for a Creator God, and no objective standard of right and wrong. It is little wonder that those of us committed to model the Master find the challenge overwhelming. There is no respect for God, no concept of sin, and when it comes to Jesus Christ, total ignorance!

But we cannot abandon our society. We have been called to bring Jesus to our generation and model Him before a society that doesn't have a clue what He is all about. *That* is our mandate! And our effectiveness is going to be determined, not by what we *say*, but by who we *are*. We *must* model our message!

When I look back and reflect on where I was twenty years ago, it is difficult to quantify the change that has come to my life. A twenty-year hiatus, a lonely journey through my own wilderness, came to an end when Evelyn and I remarried in 2004 on what would have been our forty-fifth wedding anniversary. Remarriage is not for everyone, but for us, it has been to our strength. God has blessed our home, but more importantly, we have grown and matured in our walk with God.

God has been good to me and out of the darkness initiated the dawning of a new day. *The Making of a Model* is more than a convenient title to this book; it is the story of my life. Living as a long-haul trucker, a lonely existence when it was, literally, just "Jesus and me," was as much a modeling opportunity as were my years in active ministry. Life is not all peaches and cream; sometimes, our modeling is done amid life's most difficult circumstances.

II. The Image of God

Although the modeling process is a spiritual endeavor, we model the Master with the totality of our being. Our manner of life—our drives, predispositions, and spiritual endeavors—are *all* meant to reflect the majesty of our God.

In 1 Thessalonians. 5:23, the Apostle Paul seems to think of our human nature as consisting of three distinct elements: body, soul, and spirit. "May your whole spirit, soul and body be kept blameless at the coming of our Lord." And, likewise, the writer to the Hebrews indicates much the same when he writes of the "word of God is living and active ... it penetrates even to dividing soul and spirit, joints and marrow." (Heb. 4:12).

Because the Scriptures seldom differentiate between soul and spirit, theologians are divided on whether to think of man as a two-element being consisting of a material body and an immaterial soul and spirit, or, as I have postulated, a being made up of three distinct elements. In my view, we are spirit beings with a soul living in a body.

I have postulated man as a three-part being because of the influence it has on our modeling mandate. If we are to represent the Master effectively, if the world is to get a true picture of who He is, we must serve as living models in all three aspects of our nature.

> Man is created in the image and likeness of God. God is Spirit; He created man a spirit being with a soul that lives in a body. The spirit of man died when Adam and Eve ate the forbidden fruit, but at the acceptance of Jesus Christ as the Lord and the Saviour of life, the Holy Spirit of God comes in and restores life to (regenerate, renew) the otherwise dead spirit of man. … It is the work of the Holy Spirit to help you become like Jesus Christ, to restore man to the image and the likeness of God" (Igwe, *Following Jesus,* Discourse 6/The Spirit, Para. 2).

The *body* is the material element of our constitution. It is here that we focus on health, exercise, and self-discipline. In 1 Corinthians 6:19, the Apostle Paul writes,

> Do you not know that your body is a temple of the Holy Spirit, who is in you, whom you have received from God? You are not your own; you were bought at a price. Therefore, honor God with your body.

The *soul* speaks to our intellect and mind, our decision-making organ, the storehouse of our knowledge. It is the source of our emotions, our will, and our powers of reason; it is here we integrate our experiences in life with our understanding of reality and truth.

The *spirit* is the faculty through which we establish and maintain a relationship with God. It is the immaterial part of our being, the source of our conscience, that part of us that connects with God.

Bob Proctor put it this way:

> You live simultaneously on three different planes of life. You live in a physical body, you have an intellect, and you are a perfect spiritual expression. It necessarily follows that you communicate on all three planes simultaneously (Proctor, *12 Power Principles,* 186).

On a physical level, we communicate with our actions, emotions, and speech; on an intellectual level, we communicate by our self-discipline and the principles we live by; on a spiritual level, we communicate by our integrity and character, that is, by the person we are.

God created each of us as unique individuals, and inevitably, we will give priority to one or the other of these three facets of our personality. The progress we make in our walk with God will be determined by the extent to which we can keep each of these three elements of our nature in balance.

On the one hand, a person's primary drive may revolve around what the New Testament defines as the *flesh*. Unless people have surrendered their lives to Jesus Christ, they are focused on their physical well-being. Their interest is to enjoy life for all it has to offer; they are inclined to give little thought to their intellectual development and no thought to matters of the spirit.

The Apostle Paul has little good to say about this segment of society.

> Since they did not think it worthwhile to retain the knowledge of God, he gave them over to a depraved mind, to do what ought not to be done. They have become filled with every kind of wickedness, evil, greed and depravity. They are full of envy, murder, strife, deceit and malice. They are gossips, slanderers, God-haters, insolent, arrogant and invent ways of doing evil; they disobey their parents; they are senseless, faithless, heartless, ruthless" (Rom. 1:28-31).

On the other hand, some have been born with an inquisitive mind and for whom priority one is the pursuit of knowledge. Intelligent, self-confident, and respected, they are inclined to think through the pressures of life. Faith is difficult for them. These individuals are more likely to debate the issues, question everything, and come to Christ only after they have studied the options and determined the Christian faith makes sense.

And then there are those of us who have surrendered our lives to Christ and found the primary motivating force in our life has to do with matters of the spirit. We take the stewardship of our body and mind seriously, but spiritual growth and a vibrant relationship with God have become priority one. We identify with the Apostle Paul when he writes,

> If you live according to the sinful nature, you will die; but if by the Spirit you put to death the misdeeds of the body, you will live, because those who are led by the Spirit of God are

sons of God ... The Spirit himself testifies with our spirit that we are God's children (Rom. 8:13-14, 16).

The point of this discussion is that, thanks to God's creative genius, each of us is an exclusive, one-of-a-kind individual. We come to the table with our own history, strengths, and predispositions. Even within the family of God, we have athletes and academics, tradesmen and architects, performers, and yes, writers too. We all, however, need each other, and we each have something to contribute to the orderly progress of society.

And if we are believers, all of us have one thing in common: our commitment to Christ. Our differences are to our strength, giving each of us a unique role in God's Kingdom. In our diversity, we model the Master in a way not possible by anyone else.

This concept of modeling our faith on every level of our being is well illustrated by Maggie Gobran, often called the Mother Teresa of Egypt.

I became acquainted with Maggie Gobran at the 2011 internationally televised Global Leadership Summit, sponsored by the Chicago, Illinois Willow Creek Community Church. Maggie Gobran was one of the featured speakers, and she made an impression few of us attending the conference will ever forget.

At the conclusion of her remarks, Mama Gobran, as she is affectionately known, made this comment:

> Silence your words so that you may listen to your thoughts;
> Silence your thoughts so that you may listen to your heart;
> Silence your heart so that you may listen to God.

And then, resplendent in her all-white habit, she said, "I would like to end my presentation by thanking God and blessing you." And then, kneeling to the carpet, face in her hands against the floor, Mama Gobran spent the next five minutes in silent prayer. There wasn't a dry eye in the house as several hundred pastors, and church leaders watched in awe, profoundly moved as the benevolent "Mother of Cairo" prayed for us. It was a moment to be remembered.

Mama Gobran is an apt example of what I'm writing about.

She was raised in wealth and already successful in the business world when a personal visit to the garbage slums servicing the city of Cairo touched her heart. She soon recruited an army of men and women who shared her vision and founded Steven's Children.

A manufacturing center that gave many of her kid's marketable skills soon followed, along with schools, medical clinics, and homes for children abandoned by their families. A new world was opened to hundreds of young people who had no clue how they were going to break the chains of poverty and hopelessness in which they had been trapped. Thanks to Mama Gobran, over 30,000 families are reported to have been blessed with God's love.

Never before has the chorus we used to sing been more true.

> What the world needs is Jesus, just a glimpse of Him."
> He will bring joy and gladness; take away sin and sadness.
> What the world needs is Jesus; just a glimpse of Him.

So true ... and yet, in a day when sin is rampant and God's Word is never read, society's only access to Jesus is through men and women like you and me, ministering to every level of need, materially, intellectually, *and* spiritually.

We are the only Bible most people will ever read, the only Jesus they will ever know. To serve as living models of the Master is more than a carefully designed objective; it is, in fact, what the Christian life is all about.

> You are the light of the world. ... let your light shine before men, that they may see your good deeds and praise your Father in heaven (Matt. 5:15-16).

I make a point of this because, if we are to impact our society, we must model the Master in every area of our being, body, soul, and spirit. And we must minister, in turn, to every level of need, materially, intellectually, *and* spiritually. *That* is our mission.

For the Christian community, that is a daunting challenge. America has turned away from God and chosen to ignore the basic principles of morality and godliness given us in His Word. The only Jesus they will ever know, it would seem, is the Jesus they see in us; and the only the Bible they will ever read, is the revelation of God's truth they see exemplified by our lives.

Our mission is clear cut. As never before in the history of mankind, society needs to see men and women like you and me, serving as living models of Jesus Christ.

– Strategies for Living #5 –

Gone ... but Never Forgotten

Talk of unsung heroes, outstanding men who were largely ignored and soon forgotten, and Joseph, Jesus' stepfather, goes to the top of my list.

The last we hear of Joseph is in the Gospel of Luke, Chapter 2, where we read that Jesus' "father" was present on a journey the family made to Jerusalem when Jesus was twelve years old. Even then, Joseph is not named. That's it! We never hear of him again, not even as to his death. He may have been gone, but he was never forgotten.

Much has been made of Mary, and rightly so. She was a special woman given a role second to no one else in the annals of history. We can only imagine what a moving experience it must have been the first time she looked into the face of her precious baby and realized she was looking at the face of God!

But she was not alone. For Joseph, also, it was an incredible experience. As head of the family, it fell to Joseph to give Jesus the stability and the security He needed as a child. During his teen years, Jesus watched as Joseph managed the affairs of their home. Jesus' understanding of truth and honesty, self-discipline, morality, respect for authority, and godliness were all influenced by what He observed in the man he called "Dad." He watched as Joseph responded to the frustrations and challenges of managing a business in first-century Israel. It was, undoubtedly, a critical factor in His education.

Keep in mind that Joseph was a normal man. He, like each of us, needed to discover the strength of character that can be developed only through the give and take of life. There were undoubtedly times when he blew it, and perhaps occasions when he didn't respond well to the growing-up antics of his unique stepson. But he was a good man, and God Himself chose him for the rearing of His beloved Son.

Although history records little of Jesus' childhood, one can surmise Jesus also saw Joseph smile and relax, as together they spent many quiet afternoons fishing and enjoying each other's company. What an impact the many conversations they had together must have made on Jesus' outlook on life! Joseph, as no other man on earth, helped make Jesus the man He was to become.

It is a lesson we all need to take to heart. If we are typical, we develop our self-respect, indeed, our very attitude toward life, by the things we own and the success we have experienced. We admire wealth, power, and fame. God, however, seems to have a very different agenda. He is far more interested in who we *are* than in what we *do*. Character is primary!

Our accomplishments may be limited. We may be unknown and unheralded. No one may ever squabble over our estate. But much like Joseph, that does not determine our worth. The impact of the life we have lived will be seen in the lives of the family for whom we have been made responsible. As they follow in our footsteps, as they honor the God they have met through our example, then will our worth and the impact of our lives become evident. Our living will not have been in vain!

– 9 –

The Battle for the Bible
The Inspired Word of God

*You will know the truth and
the truth will set you free.*

John 8:32

THE YEAR WAS 1949, and two young evangelists were about to launch a crusade in Los Angeles, California. It was an endeavor that would have a historic and deeply personal impact on them and the church.

Charles Templeton, who had been preaching on alternating nights with his best friend, Billy Graham, was in the throes of a spiritual crisis.

In an interview related to his book, *The Case For Faith*, Lee Strobel tells of a conversation he had with Templeton not long before Charles' death in 2001.

> "Was there one thing in particular that caused you to lose your faith in God?" I asked at the outset.
>
> He thought for a moment, "It was a photograph in Life magazine," he said finally.
>
> "Really?" I said. "A photograph? How so?"
>
> He narrowed his eyes a bit and looked off to the side, as if he were viewing the photo afresh and reliving the moment. "It was a picture of a black woman in Northern Africa," he explained. "They were experiencing a devastating drought. And she was holding her dead baby in her arms and looking up to heaven with the most forlorn expression. I looked at it and I thought, 'Is it possible to believe that there is a loving or caring Creator when all this woman needed was rain?'" (14).

It was a question that would have a devastating impact on Templeton's faith in the Bible, and he made no secret of his feelings. As Graham recounts in his autobiography, *Just As I Am,* Templeton challenged him. "Billy," he said, "you're fifty years out of date. People no longer accept the Bible as being inspired the way you do. Your faith is too simple" (138). Billy Graham, who had enormous respect for his friend, could not dismiss Templeton's argument out of hand. "If I was not exactly doubtful," he recalled, "I was certainly disturbed" (138).

Things finally came to a head for Graham during a quiet walk in the San Bernardino mountains.

> Dropping to my knees there in the woods, I opened the Bible at random on a tree stump in front of me. I could not read it in the shadowy moonlight, so I had no idea what text lay

9 – The Battle for the Bible

before me. ... [I]t was an altar where I could only stutter into prayer.

The exact wording of my prayer is beyond recall, but it must have echoed my thoughts: "O God! There are many things in this book I do not understand. There are many problems with it for which I have no solution." ...

I was trying to be on the level with God, but something remained unspoken. At last the Holy Spirit freed me to say it. "Father, I am going to accept this as Thy Word—by faith! I'm going to allow faith to go beyond my intellectual questions and doubts, and I will believe this to be Your inspired Word (B. Graham, 139).

Templeton soon withdrew from the ministry, moved to Canada, and became a writer and commentator. His final published work, *Farewell to God: My Reasons for Rejecting the Christian Faith,* tells the story. For Graham, however, the Los Angeles crusade launched a ministry that was to enable hundreds of thousands of people to discover a new relationship with the God Templeton had rejected.

The decision Billy Graham made that fateful night is typical of the dilemma encountered by every Bible-believing Christian. In our quest for God, in our search for truth, our belief in the authority of God's Word raises a series of questions that can not always be easily answered. Can we trust the Bible as an unerring and infallible foundation to our faith?

Second only to belief in the death and resurrection of Jesus Christ, the authority of God's Word is the foundation principle of our faith. We have fought, and I believe, won the debate challenging Jesus' resurrection. The battle for the Bible, however, even among evangelicals, is ongoing.

I. The Search for Truth

I feel compelled to defend my understanding of the Word of God as being inerrant and infallible. I make a point of this for, if we are to model the Master, we have but one source for knowledge of the Man we are to emulate. The story of His life, the principles by which He lived, and the ensuing message of the New Testament Church we discover in and only in God's Word.

In the early days of our nation our Founding Fathers had a profound respect for the Bible and looked to it for direction in much of their deliberation. Tragically, however, as America turned away from God, the Bible lost its influence and no longer has a voice in America's public affairs.

Things have changed from the days when educators used the Bible as an introductory text in primary education. As noted by Dr. Benjamin Rush, a signer of the Declaration of Independence,

> The great enemy of the salvation of man, in my opinion, never invented a more effectual means of extirpating [extinguishing] Christianity from the world than by persuading mankind that it was improper to read the Bible at school. [T]he Bible, when not read in schools, is seldom read in any subsequent period of life. ... [It] should be read in our schools in preference to all other books from its containing [sic] the greatest portion of that kind of knowledge which is calculated to produce private and public temporal happiness (Barton, *Original Intent*, 162).

9 – The Battle for the Bible

Our society no longer reflects the profound reverence early America had for God's Word. A generation of young people, educated without respect for God and his Word, now teach our children, lead our business enterprises, and govern our land. Many of us believe it is not coincidental that we are currently struggling with social upheaval and lawlessness in America not seen since the days of the Korean War.

Our founding fathers did not want to eliminate God or His Word from our national conscience. When they drafted the First Amendment, *"Congress shall make no law respecting an establishment of religion or prohibiting the free exercise thereof..."* (Barton, 21), they did so not to minimize the influence of the Christian faith but to protect the church from governmental control.

Liberal America, however, has used the First Amendment to justify its anti-Christian bias. With the call for the separation of Church and state, the progressive left has isolated God and His Word out of our national life.

I must tell you that from my earliest days, I have looked to God for His blessing on my life. I soon learned that if I were to develop a viable relationship with God, it would be based on what I read in His Word. Accordingly then, and without question, I accepted the Word as my guide in both my faith and the manner of life it called on me to live.

For many, however, even in the evangelical church, trust in the Bible as the very Word of God has been weakened by the current debate. This is a major issue for me, for I believe the survival of the church is at stake.

The Making of a Model

The account of what happened at Fuller Seminary, Pasadena, CA, is a disturbing case in point.

Founded by Charles Fuller in 1947 as a School of Missions and Evangelism, Fuller Seminary was once the stronghold of orthodox fundamentalism. By the early 1960s, however, changes were taking place.

> Doubts began to arise on the Fuller board and faculty about the inerrancy of Scripture. ... David Hubbard was hired as president in spite of the fact that the syllabus on the Old Testament he had coauthored with Robert Laurin stated that Adam was not historical, Moses had not written the whole Pentateuch, and Daniel was written after the great world kingdom events that are recorded as prophecies in his book," (Geisler, *Defending Inerrancy*, 20-21).

But if we challenge the message and its source, if we assume the documents allegedly written by Moses or Isaiah or Daniel are bogus, we not only influence the message they had to deliver, we are challenging the wisdom and knowledge of Jesus Himself. He believed in them and their message.

> In recent times, it has been fashionable among Protestant thinkers to deny both the omniscience and infallibility of Jesus. C. H Dodd comments: "We need not doubt that Jesus, as He is represented, shared the views of His contemporaries regarding the authorship of books in the Old Testament, or the phenomena of 'demon possession' — views which we could not accept without violence to our sense of truth" (Montgomery, *God's Inerrant Word*, 275).

The result is a weakened faith supported by an emasculated Bible. If there is no such thing as the supernatural, if miracles are not genuine, if the resurrection never took place, if the New Testament is merely a record of developing legends emerging from a fledgling church, then our faith has been destroyed.

A generation of Americans, predisposed to reject the moral principles highlighted by God's Word, have found their escape by maintaining the New Testament to be little more than a record of the church's first century thought. And where did they get that idea? All too often, tragically, from the church!

And as the church goes, so goes the nation.

On June 26, 2015, the United States Supreme Court, in a case known as *Obergefell v Hodges*, held that "the right to marry is a fundamental right inherent in the liberty of the person."

> A year before the Obergefell decision, the Presbyterian Church (USA) approved homosexual marriage. ... About two weeks before the Supreme Court's decision, Tony Campolo, a well-known, outspoken Christian leader, came out in favor of gay marriage. ... Influential author and blogger Rachel Held Evans, who no longer considers herself an evangelical, offers full support for same-sex marriage, basing her position almost exclusively on feelings and a desire to affirm others rather than Scripture (Hitchcock, *The Coming Apostasy*, 116-117).

I thank God millions of Christians do not agree. For them, as for me, the Bible is *God's* Word. We have disciplined our lives by its principles, judged our actions by its directives, and sustained our faith by its promises.

The Making of a Model

The question every Christian must answer comes down to this: Is the Bible a statement of divine truth to be believed and defended as inerrant and infallible in all that it says? Or is it the *record* of a revelation, subject to modern standards of truth?

That determination is not always easy to make. Did Jonah spend three days inside the "belly of a huge fish" (Matt. 12:40)? Did Peter really walk on water? Did Jesus feed over 5,000 men and their families, all within the span of a few hours? Was Lazarus truly dead and truly brought back to life? I believe so; such truths form the foundation of my faith.

This is not "trivial pursuit," and we are not playing games here. On this truth—that the Bible as we have it is the very word of God—hangs the survival of our faith. If the Bible is not an unerring guide in both our faith and practice, the message of the Church is invalid and without foundation. But not to worry. God has given us a sure and faithful guide we can trust with our lives, and the truths of God's Word are, in fact, its own best defense.

In October 1978, the International Council on Biblical Inerrancy held a summit near O'Hare Airport. The result was the *Chicago Statement on Biblical Inerrancy*. As outlined in a book by Norman Geisler and William Roach, *Defending Inerrancy* (26-30), I accept the Chicago Statement and summarize my view in my own words as follows.

1. The Scriptures, being God's Word and written by men prepared and directed by His Spirit, are of infallible divine

authority in all matters on which it touches, including faith, science, and history.

2. The Bible is, in its entirety, a revelation given by God and is without error or fault in all its teaching. We can trust its literary origins under God and believe as true what it states about God's acts in creation, the events of world history, and its witness to God's saving grace in individual lives.

3. The whole of Scripture in all its parts, including the very words of the original, were given by divine inspiration.

4. The Scriptures are infallible and inerrant, free from falsehood, dishonesty, or deception. All claims of the Bible must correspond with reality, whether that reality is historical, factual, or spiritual.

5. The authors of Scripture were writing to an audience of their times and must be understood in light of what they had to say to their contemporaries.

6. Divine inspiration, though not conferring omniscience, guaranteed true and trustworthy utterance on all matters of which the Biblical authors were moved to speak and write.

In summary, the Sacred Scriptures have been for me, not a word from God, subject to my predispositions, but the word *of* God, unalterable, inerrant, and inspired by God's Holy Spirit. Faithful men, writing to their contemporaries, delivered a message with prophetic overtones they themselves may not have always understood, but which was, in fact, God's love letter to His people.

II. Inspiration and the Authority of God's Word

My belief in the authority of God's Word stems from the conviction that although the words of Scripture are the words of men, they are words that were inspired by the Holy Spirit. *Theopneustos*, the Greek word for *inspiration* as used in 2 Tim. 3:16, means *God-breathed*.

> All scripture is God-breathed ["inspired of God" (ASV)] and is useful for teaching, rebuking correction, and training in righteousness, so that the man of God may be thoroughly equipped for every good work (2 Tim. 3:16-17).

The Apostle Peter agrees.

> Prophecy never had its origin in the will of man, but men spoke from God as they were carried along by the Holy Spirit (2 Pet. 1:21).

Inspiration may be defined as a supernatural influence whereby the Spirit of God assures us of the trustworthiness of both the written and oral proclamation given us through specially chosen Prophets and Apostles (see Unger, *Bible Dictionary*, 620). It is not that the Scriptures are seen as a human product inspired or breathed by the Spirit of God, but a divine product produced by inspired authors who were men of their times.

Even more so than its inspiration, the primary concern for the Biblical authors was the Scriptures' authority. As they delivered their message, both the Prophets and the Apostles were concerned that their proclamation be viewed as a word *from* God. They were speaking to their times in terms their times could understand, but they believed they were delivering the very words of God.

> The first claim to be made for Scripture is not its inerrancy nor even its inspiration, but its authority. Standing in the forefront of prophetic-apostolic proclamation is the divine authority of Scripture as the Word of God (Henry IV, *God*, 27).

Both the Prophets and the Apostles were concerned that their proclamation be viewed as a word *from* God. They were speaking to their times in terms their times could understand, but they believed they were delivering the very words of God.

The Apostles saw themselves as standing in the same relationship with God as did the Prophets and referred back to the Prophets to support their message. It enabled them to understand what God was doing or about to do through Jesus and His Church.

It is sometimes difficult for us to realize the men God chose to pen and proclaim His revelation were ordinary, fallible human beings who were frequently questioned and despised by their own people. They didn't enjoy the veneration we give them today. Zechariah was "stoned to death in the courtyard of the Lord's temple" (2 Chron. 24:21); the Prophet Isaiah was "sawed in two" (Heb. 11:37). And even the Apostle Paul, as important as he was to the New Testament church, languished in prison, abandoned even by his friends in his final days.

What made these men outstanding in the plan of God was not their popular appeal. Their message and their writings, however, were inspired by the Holy Spirit. God used them, and He did so within the context of their own weaknesses, personalities, and character.

The Apostle Peter put it this way.

> And we have the word of the prophets made more certain, and you will do well to pay attention to it, as to a light shining in a dark place, until the day dawns and the morning star rises in your hearts. Above all, you must understand that no prophecy of Scripture came about by the prophet's own interpretation. For prophecy never had its origin in the will of man, but men spoke from God as they were carried along by the Holy Spirit (2 Peter 1:19-21).

I will grant the position I have taken raises some thorny questions. Old Testament miracles, the history of the people of Israel, and predictive prophecy as given by Isaiah, Ezekiel, and Daniel, all challenge believability.

And the challenging issues to which I refer are not restricted to the Old Testament. The Gospels, penned from four different points of view, bring up several apparent contradictions.

As a case in point, I note that Mark indicates Jesus was crucified the day after He celebrated Passover with His disciples (Mark 14:12; 15:25). John, however, writes that Jesus died on the Day of Preparation, the day before the Passover meal was eaten (John 19:14).

A solution to the difference between the two reports is clarified by Dwight Pentecost, writing in *The Word and Works of Jesus Christ*.

The Galileans and Pharisees used the sunrise to sunrise reckoning whereas the Judeans and Sadducees used the sunset to sunset reckoning. Thus, according to the Synoptics, the Last Supper was a Passover meal. Since the day was reckoned from sunrise, the Galileans, and with them Jesus and His disciples, had the Paschal lamb slaughtered in the late afternoon of Thursday, Nisan 14, and later that evening they ate the Passover with the unleavened bread. On the other hand, the Judean Jews who reckoned from sunset to sunset would slay the lamb on Friday afternoon which marked the end of Nisan 14 and would eat the Passover lamb with the unleavened bread that night which had become Nisan 15. Thus, Jesus had eaten the Passover meal when His enemies, who had not as yet had the Passover, arrested Him (421).

Mark and John were working with two different calendars and the meal was a Passover meal, held the day *before* Passover was celebrated in Jerusalem. This is significant for it means that Jesus, the lamb of God, died at the same time the Paschal lambs were being slain in the temple precincts.

III. Inerrancy and the Infallibility of God's Word

In a day when truth has been declared relative and morality a matter of choice, it is imperative that we once again recognize God's Word as the supreme, written authority on issues of both faith and practice. Indeed, the Bible is a magnificent work of literature, but it is more, much more than that. As delivered by the original authors to the people of their day, it was and is the very Word of God, without error and true in all that it states.

That premise has been challenged by secular society and increasingly by people from within the Christian community. It is difficult for people, taught from their earliest days that all truth is subjective, to accept the premise that the Bible, although written over a period of fifteen hundred years, can be trusted as being consistent with reality and fact.

Irregularities in grammar or spelling are not an issue here. Astounding descriptions of nature — of the sun standing still, the ax-head floating, three men walking out of a fiery furnace, water becoming wine, or a man like Peter walking on water — do not negate the truthfulness of either the Old or New Testament record. These events raise thorny questions I cannot always answer to my satisfaction, but I have determined I will accept by faith even those issues God has not chosen to clarify in terms I can understand. *The authors wrote of these events as factual*, and I accept them as true.

Indeed, I am convinced the Bible can be trusted, whatever the issue, including ethics, history, and science, a position known as *unlimited inerrancy*. I do not accept the premise that inspiration relates only to matters of faith, sometimes termed *limited inerrancy*. On the contrary, I believe the Bible to be true on all issues the authors of Scripture wrote to their contemporaries.

I make a point of this, for I believe it imperative that we support and defend *both* the inerrancy and the infallibility of God's Word. Although the terms are sometimes used interchangeably, there are differences in emphasis, and those differences

9 – The Battle for the Bible

make it critical that we maintain their corresponding distinction.

Carl F. H. Henry, writing in *God, Revelation and Authority, Vol IV*, notes the subtle difference between the terms.

> *Infallible* "signifies the quality of neither misleading nor being misled and so safeguards in categorical terms the truth that the Scriptures are a sure, safe, and reliable rule and guide in all matters." Similarly, *inerrant* "signifies the quality of being free from all falsehood or mistake and so safeguards the truth that Holy Scripture is entirely true and trustworthy in all its assertions" (217).

I am not surprised at the pre-disposition of non-believers to question the Scriptures. Their autonomy, the liberty to live as they please, is at stake. But there is no excuse for a Church that was "called out of darkness into His marvelous light" (1 Pet. 2:9) to question the reliability of the Biblical record. We claim to stand for truth, but truth, it seems, has all too often been sacrificed in favor of society's approval. If the Church is to survive as the voice of God to contemporary society, we must acknowledge its divine origin and accept it as a trustworthy guide in all that it states.

In February 2019, the United Methodist denomination convened the "Special Session of the General Conference of The United Methodist Church" in St. Louis, MO. With broad support from overseas representatives, conservative delegates at the conference defeated a plan that would have allowed LGBT clergy and same-sex marriage within the United Methodist Church. Fifty-six percent of the eight hundred delegates supported what conservatives called *The*

Traditional Plan. It upholds the church's stance prohibiting LGBT members from being ordained and does not permit same-sex couples to be married by the Church.

Significantly, forty-four percent of the delegates supported overturning the ban. It is tragic, that the United Methodist fellowship, once the mainstay of orthodox theology, is being threatened with a split over an issue about which the Scriptures are clear and beyond doubt.

> Do you not know that the wicked will not inherit the kingdom of God? Do not be deceived. Neither the sexually immoral nor idolaters nor adulterers nor male prostitutes nor homosexual offenders nor thieves nor the greedy nor drunkards nor slanderers nor swindlers will inherit the kingdom of God (1 Cor. 6:9-10).

But all is not lost. Despite an institutional church that has questioned its source of authority and redefined its message, God has reserved for Himself a multitude of people like you and me, blood-bought and Spirit-filled, committed to defend and champion the message of His Word.

God has given us the truth of His Word, the power of His Spirit, and the fellowship of like-minded believers that we might serve our generation as effective, living models of the Master!

– Strategies for Living #6 –
The Tapestry of My Life

Cusco, Peru, at the time a small Andean town of some sixty thousand inhabitants, was for me, the son of missionary parents, just home. A city with only one respectable hotel and no fine restaurants, Cusco in the late 1940s wasn't anything like the tourist mecca it has become today. What stands out, however, and the thought behind this article, is the outstanding piece of clothing quite common among the natives, the poncho. The truly native-woven ponchos smelled of smoke, hand-woven as they were in their modest homes, of wool from their own sheep.

But they were fine pieces of clothing nonetheless, made up of sheep's wool in finely woven hues of red and blue and yellow and green. Magnificent!

I refer to the poncho for it is, in a sense, a metaphor of my life.

In eighty-two years of living, my journey has had moments of ecstasy and moments of despair, times when I was brilliant and times when I looked the fool, times when I made my family proud, and those other times they would have rather thrown me out with the garbage. I am neither bragging nor complaining, but I do wish to make a point: highs and lows come with living. They go with our human nature.

But I am encouraged, for my Bible says "all things work together for good to them.... who are called according to His purpose." (Rom. 8:28, KJV) God may not have been pleased with my mistakes nor approved of my willful antics, but He has proven to be more than able to take them and *of them*, to quote the Prophet Isaiah, produce a "garment of praise" (Isa. 61:3).

It may come as a surprise to know that God can take a life that is as checkered as mine and of it make something of beauty. Yes ... He takes all of life ... our sins, our mistakes, our errors of judgment, and even our failures ... and, given our cooperation, weaves them together to make of us a magnificent reflection of His creative genius. The final product we see in Jesus; He was what we have been created to be!

You may wonder at that, for Christians are far from perfect. The tapestry of our lives includes the good, the bad, and sometimes even the ugly. But we have been forgiven, we have been taken over by a merciful God, and He is in the process of making of us something we could never hope to become without Him: living models of the Master Himself. Only God could make that kind of a call, and only God can make it happen. But it *can* happen, and it can happen to *you*.

PART FOUR

The Making of a Model

Our human tendency is to focus on our calling — on where we should go, how we should get there, and what exactly we should do about it. God's concern is the process that he is taking us through to mature us and ready us, making us more like his Son. All of us... are works in process.

~ Chuck Swindoll ~

… 10 …

Modeling the Master Begins at Home
Marriage … as it was Supposed to Be

Each one of you must love his wife as he loves himself,
and the wife must respect her husband.

Ephesians 5:33

SO FAR IN THIS TREATISE we have looked at the Perfect Model … the prototype of who and what we were created to be. We have taken the time to point to His life, His death, and His resurrection as proof of his deity and as providing the divine pattern we are called to emulate. As we are told in 1 Pet. 2:20-21,

> If you suffer for doing good and you endure it, this is commendable before God. To this you were called, because Christ suffered for you, leaving you an example that you should follow in his steps.

But that brings up this question: where and how do we initiate the "following" process? And the answer is simple and yet quite profound: modeling the Master begins at home.

Most of us spent our childhood years under the authority and leadership of our parents. From them, it is hoped, we learned the principles that would guide us for life. During our teen years the responsibility shifted. As we aged it slowly became our responsibility to decide how we would apply or reject the principles of responsible living they instilled in us.

Barring a total rejection of everything our parents stood for and presupposing the example of their lives was a valid model for us to follow, things went reasonably well until we hit college. There we most likely encountered an assault on everything we believed. Morality, truth, conduct, right and wrong, in short, everything we should have been taught was up for debate. This was a decisive time for each of us, a turning point, our moment of truth. It was to impact our relationship with God, our choice of a career, and for most of us, our selection of a mate.

And then we married, with all the hopes and exciting plans typical of this phase of life. The honeymoon, however, was soon over, and our relationship precipitated a wake-up call that opened our eyes to a new reality: marriage is tough!

> Christians who dodge all serious struggles and consciously seek to put themselves in whatever situation and relationships are easiest ... are coasting, and eventually that coasting will define them and—even worse—shape them. ... [A] good marriage is not something you find, it is something you work for. It takes struggle. You must crucify your

selfishness. ... This is undeniably hard work! But eventually, it pays off. Eventually, it creates a relationship of beauty, trust, and mutual support (Thomas, *Sacred Marriage*, 133).

In short, marriage will drive us to distraction, or it will drive us to God.

I. My Self: The Last Idol to Fall

Almost without exception, every intra-personal conflict comes down to the issue of self, called "the flesh" in Scripture. It is true that alcohol, drugs, immorality, and other outside forces may have impacted the life God has for us. But that's not at issue here; our problem is that even in healthy relationships, *self* demands command and control.

A. The Drive for Supremacy

The dominance of self-serving drives and ambitions will stay with us throughout our lifetime. But the *self*, more commonly known as the *ego*, can be put in its proper place. It humbles and distresses me to discover that after years of prayer, self-discipline, and living by my Christian convictions, my *self* is still clamoring for satisfaction.

I was, of course, born that way. Within just a few moments of birth, and thanks to a doctor who thought I needed a wake-up call, he slapped me sharply on the backside. And I was quick to let the world know what I thought of him and everyone else in the room. I began life demanding my way, and although restricted by common sense, my parents, and the law, I have been demanding my will prevail ever since.

It is easy to understand the fundamental problem here when you factor in the influence of my *self*—self-ambition, self-image, and self-will. Dealing with *self* is tough. My predisposition is to play the fiddle and hope the rest of the world will dance to my tune. But it cannot, and it must not, be.

The reason is simple. None of us can get along on the job, enjoy a happy marriage, or raise a family of children unless our inner self is disciplined and put in its place. *Self*—the flesh—is the essence of sin. *My way* and *God's way* have been in conflict since the days of Adam and Eve. And it is here we discover why most people resist submission to the Lordship of Jesus Christ: we want control; we don't want anyone, even God, to tell us how to live. Even after surrendering our life to Christ our self-centeredness keeps coming back to the surface for a new breath of fresh air. We never tire of demanding our own way. The process of unlearning self and learning Christ is a difficult process for all of us. Ambition, pride, and self-confidence, all necessary to survival in our competitive society, must nevertheless be sanctified by the Spirit of God if we are to serve as effective living models of the Master.

Modeling the Master begins right here. Surrendering our lives to Jesus Christ marks our point of departure. In doing so, however, we have launched a battle with our *self* that will last a lifetime. And self dies hard. It is, indeed, the last enemy in the believer's life to be destroyed. It seems that we will sacrifice anything, give anything, do anything if our *self* can remain pacified and in control.

Not only is this a never-ending battle, but it is also *the* battle of the Christian life.

B. The Subjugation of the Flesh

So then, what are we to do? How are we to deal with the flesh when we still want to have our own way? The Apostle Paul, writing in Gal. 5:14, is direct and to the point, "So I say, *live by the Spirit,* and you will not gratify the desires of the sinful nature."

This is critical, for I believe there is no way we will be able to model the Master without suppressing the flesh, and for that, we need the power and leadership of God's Holy Spirit.

It is clear from Rom. 8:9 that all God's children receive the indwelling presence of the Holy Spirit from the moment of his or her conversion. It is the Spirit's convicting power that brings us into the family of God. That, however, is only a beginning; there is more, much more, the Holy Spirit would like to do in our lives.

I would have long ago surrendered any hope of success in my battle with pride, self-ambition and sin were it not for my confidence in the power and work of God's Spirit. The longer I serve the Lord, the more conscious I have become of my need for the active, empowering presence of the Holy Spirit in my life.

> If you live according to the sinful nature, you will die; but if by the Spirit you put to death the misdeeds of the body, you will live, because those who are led by the Spirit of God are the sons of God (Rom. 8:13-14).

I wish I could tell you that, having joined the fight for better than eighty years, I have been able to bring my self-centered inclinations under control. I was hoping that as I aged, the conflict with sin and self would be minimized. But such has not been the case. I have, however, made significant progress and I have discovered that so long as I keep my focus on my relationship with Jesus Christ, self remains under control.

And I am not alone. Read Romans 7, and you will see that the Apostle Paul knew what I am going through.

> I find this law at work: When I want to do good, evil is right there with me. For in my inner being I delight in God's law; but I see another law at work in the members of my body, waging war against the law of my mind, and making me a prisoner of the law of sin at work within my members. What a wretched man I am! Who will rescue me from this body of death? Thanks be to God—through Jesus Christ our Lord! (Rom. 7:21-25).

It may, at first glance, seem that I am off track from the theme of this chapter. If we are to model the Master, however, that modeling process reaches its most challenging moment in marriage and the Christian home. And I am not being cynical. Two ego-centric people, each wanting to have their own way, each battling their own problems with self and sin, soon discover how explosive even a good relationship can be. It is here we will need the leadership and power of the Holy Spirit working with us and through us as at no other time in life.

II. Marriage: Becoming One in Christ

It is tragic that, even among evangelicals, I must define what I mean by *marriage* and on this God's word is clear.

Marriage is a loving and loyal relationship between one man and one woman.

Jesus, with reference to the creation of Adam and Eve (Gen. 1:26-28), stated,

> "Haven't you read," he replied, "that at the beginning the Creator 'made them male and female,' and said, 'For this reason a man will leave his father and mother and be united to his wife, and the two will become one flesh?'" (Matt. 19:4-5).

Here there can be no debate.

God has designed the home so that every child has access to a father with the courage to discipline and demand respect and a sympathizing mother with a soft heart. Each parent has a critical role to play; they complement each other.

Tragically, however, society and circumstances have compromised the role of the family unit. Every child needs the influence of both a mother *and* a father; this is the heartbreak of single-parent homes, and with them, I sympathize. My concern here, however, is that it is also becoming more common in America for the home to be under the mandate of a same-sex couple. And the trouble here is not that the state has given same-sex couples the right to marry; the trouble is that *society* has determined homosexuality and gay marriage are morally acceptable.

> There have been periods in history when homosexuality has flourished, as in the biblical cities of Sodom and Gomorrah, in Greece, and in the Roman Empire. None of these civilizations survived. ... We can see where it leads by observing the Scandinavian nations of Norway, Denmark, and Sweden, whose leaders embraced de facto marriages between homosexuals in the nineties. The consequences for traditional families have been devastating. The institution of marriage in these countries is rapidly dying, with most young couples cohabiting or choosing to remain single. In some areas of Norway, 80 percent of firstborn children are conceived out of wedlock (Dobson, *Marriage Under Fire*, 8, 9).

Our society may not want to hear it, but gay marriage is an aberrant substitute for the institution of marriage as God established it in the Garden of Eden. Like so much of the devil's handiwork, gay marriage negates the commission God gave to both Adam (Gen. 1:22) and Noah (Gen. 9:1). "Be fruitful," they were told, "and multiply."

A. God's Forum for Growth

But there is more to the home than procreation and mutual support. This is *God's primary arena for our growth and maturity.*

As already stated, the quest for supremacy, the drive to have our own way, is the source of almost all our conflicts in marriage. Call it self-centeredness, ego, or pride, but whatever you term it, it devastates a healthy relationship.

My wife and I entered into marriage with such high hopes it surprised us to discover we had married into a relationship that was far from perfect. We came with different agendas, undisclosed weaknesses, and personality quirks that surfaced only after we started living together.

10 – Modeling the Master Begins at Home

As if that didn't make our marriage tough enough, we entered marriage with sinful tendencies that had no place in our lives and home.

> Behind virtually every case of marital dissatisfaction lies unrepented sin. Couples don't fall out of love so much as they fall out of repentance. Sin, wrong attitudes, and personal failures that are not dealt with slowly erode the relationship. ... All of us enter marriage with sinful attitudes. Many marriages end in divorce largely because one or both partners are running from their own revealed weaknesses as much as they are running from something they can't tolerate in their spouse (Thomas, *Sacred Marriage*, 96, 97).

Had Adam and Eve never fallen, we would each be perfect, and adjusting to our differences would have been a pleasure. But, unfortunately, most of us came into marriage with self-centered predispositions and demands that no spouse could meet, no matter how gifted and willing they might be.

For most of us, marriage has served as a wake-up call. It is here we discover the character flaws, self-centeredness, and anti-Christian attitudes that threaten to destroy our call to model the Master. God designed marriage, it seems, to challenge our immaturity and bring us, sometimes under great stress, to a place of surrender to the divine will. Marriage is God's institution. It is, hands down, the most challenging and yet most rewarding of all human relationships.

B. The Biblical Foundation

In Ephesians 5, the Apostle Paul gave us the Biblical principles that are to guide us toward a godly marriage. He begins in verse 1 by highlighting the fact that if we are to model the Master, this is where we must start.

> Be imitators of God, therefore, as dearly loved children, and live a life of love, just as Christ loved us and gave himself up for us as a fragrant offering and sacrifice to God (5:1).

And then, in verses 22 – 27, he makes this well-known statement:

> Wives, submit to your husbands as to the Lord. For the husband is the head of the wife as Christ is the head of the church, his body, of which he is the Savior. Now as the church submits to Christ, so also wives should submit to their husbands in everything. Husbands, love your wives, just as Christ loved the church and gave himself up for her, and to present her to himself ... holy and blameless.

Although men have sometimes used the divine mandate as a cover for a domineering, abusive personality, that is not what Paul is saying. He is calling us to model the Master, to serve our families with the same love and tenderness with which Jesus served His church. But most men do not come into marriage with that attitude. We live in a fallen world, and we been influenced in some way by the reality of the fall.

Gentlemen, we are God's representatives to our family. Much, if not most, of the problems we face in marriage and rearing our families stem from a breakdown right here: we have failed to reflect the holiness, patience, self-discipline,

10 – Modeling the Master Begins at Home

love, and understanding our calling demands. We may not be up to the challenge, we may have our own demons to fight, we may find ourselves in a less-than-satisfying relationship, but our calling, gentlemen, is to model the Master, *no matter what!*

C. To Each His Own

In Ephesians 5:33, summing up everything he had just stated, the Apostle Paul wrote, "Each of you also must love his wife as he loves himself, and the wife must respect her husband."

Dr. Emerson Eggerichs says that when he discovered this truth it revolutionized his theology.

> When this illustration from Scripture exploded in my heart and mind one day in 1998, it simply blew me away. I literally exclaimed, 'Glory to God!' ... What was the secret? Actually, it was no secret at all. This passage of Scripture has been there for some two thousand years for all of us to see. ... Paul is clearly saying that wives need love and husbands need respect. ... As I wrestled with the problem, I finally saw a connection: without love from him, she reacts without respect; without respect from her, he reacts without love. Around and around it goes. I call it the Crazy Cycle (Eggerichs, *Love and Respect,* 14-15, 6).

It seems simplistic, but there is here a directive that taken seriously, would revolutionize most marriages.

I say that with this caveat: if a person will adopt the Biblical model, he or she must do so as an act of surrender and obedience to Jesus Christ without preconditions or expectations, determined to stay the course regardless of how his or

The Making of a Model

her spouse reacts. This simple, common-sense formula, which sounds so good on paper, will be far from easy to apply. And let me warn you: it will take time to work.

Every wife needs to know that her husband considers her as remarkable today as she was to him during courtship. Rearing a family, dealing with the pressures in the home and on the job will often leave her drained and on edge. She deserves a break, a sympathetic shoulder to lean on, and she surely deserves a husband sensitive to her moods and who lets her know, often and in many ways, that he loves her.

The husband, in turn, desperately wants her respect and admiration. That, however, doesn't come with the territory. Gentlemen, we must earn it. The wife will seldom respect a husband who doesn't prove he deserves it. His sensitivity to her moods, his stature as a Christian, and perhaps most important of all, his ability to control his mouth, will tell the tale. Respect comes only to those who deserve to be respected.

Most of us can see the wisdom and common sense highlighted by Eph. 5:33 but to live by such an ideal takes courage, determination, and the grace of God. A godly home is well within our reach, but we will find it only in direct proportion to our mutual surrender to each other and the principles established in God's Word.

But it *is* our forum for growth. For many of us, our home is the setting, and marriage is the relationship that drive us toward becoming an effective living model of Jesus Christ.

In her book, *Just Give Me Jesus*, Anne Graham Lotz relates that after she and her husband Danny had been married ten years, she awakened one morning "to the realization that I was in a marriage where the love had run out. ... God, in His infinite mercy and love, allowed me to struggle for almost a year. During that time, it was not Danny's shortcomings God revealed to me, but my own" (45-46).

Many of us have been there, and like Anne, can verify that God can bring warmth and love back into a struggling marriage.

My marriage came to an end in July 1984, just after our twenty-fifth wedding anniversary. Although I did my best to be a good man, I was a difficult husband and the day came when she told me, "I just can't take it anymore."

The next twenty years turned out to be as difficult as our years of marriage. God, however, was at work, gently helping us mature into the people He meant each of us to be. The nightmare of those days, the disorientation, the stomach-churning sense of failure is something I would never want to go through again. It was, however, a necessary experience if I was to become a living model of Jesus Christ.

When we remarried, on June 6, 2004, our twenty-year journey through a wilderness of loneliness and despair left us remarkably different from the two young people who had married forty-five years earlier. The years of isolation and trauma had not been wasted.

An insight into the changes that have come into my life can, perhaps, be best understood from "my life's mission." I have been saying the difficult twenty-year odyssey, my wilderness experience as I have termed it, has prompted growth and self-understanding I could have discovered in no other way. It has given a positive twist to my journey, and to make sure I don't miss the point, I have developed a mission statement. Enclosed is a summary, a statement I review every day as part of my morning devotions.

MY LIFE'S MISSION

My mission, from this day forward, is to model the Master —

In my actions, my words, my discipline, my dreams, and my work, and,

To give God, unconditionally and without reservation,

The gift of a holy life,

Knowing that in all things God works for the good of those who love Him, who have been called according to His purpose.

WITH THIS STRATEGY TOWARD A SUCCESSFUL MISSION

To magnify the Lord through my life, my writing, and if and when they materialize, my speaking engagements, documenting my life's journey as the means God has used to make me a living model of Jesus Christ;

To give Evelyn the peace and happiness that has eluded her during our years of marriage, showing my love by supporting and encouraging her in those things important to her; and,

To set an example for my family by modeling a mature, self-disciplined, sanctified life they can emulate.

God has honored that commitment and blessed us in ways that, to us, are almost beyond belief. I have in my office a cherished plaque that means more to me than any gift ever received from Evelyn. It says,

> I can't promise that I'll be here for the rest of your life,
> But I can promise that I'll love you for the rest of mine.

The transition from where we were to where we are today is tantamount to a miracle. I am yet to become the man Evelyn thought she married, but the trauma of the last sixty-two years has not been wasted. Evelyn is, indeed, the best thing that ever happened to me, a gift from God given me that, slowly but surely, I might become …

A living model of Jesus Christ.

– Strategies for Living #7 –
Life in the Trenches

If you could live your life over again, would you? Most of us, without further thought, would say, "Absolutely!" But are you sure? Do you think you would be happy being the person you were thirty years ago?

Each of us is the product of our past. We are who we are today because of the circumstances, experiences, and influences that have left their mark on our lives. If we could tailor-make our past, what would we do differently? Probably nothing, for our perspective has been determined by our journey, and without that journey, we would not be the person we are today.

We all have a past, and we only go around once. We can wish all we want, but it won't change a thing. To be mired in self-pity, to give up on life, to dream of what might have been, will get us nowhere. We must face the facts, deal with the heartache, recover from our mistakes, and build on the lessons learned.

Seldom has the issue of rethinking the past been more important than it was to those who had called for Jesus' crucifixion. But something had happened in Jerusalem that changed everything; within days of the crucifixion, a report began to circulate that could not be ignored. Like it or not, they had to account for an empty tomb, eye-witnesses who claimed to have seen Him, and a group of disciples with a change of attitude. What to do?

They could ignore the issue altogether and get on with their lives. They could follow the example of the religious establishment and presume, without warrant, that the disciples had stolen His body. But they knew better, and they knew that no man will ever recover from his mistakes by claiming ignorance or by denying what he knows to be true.

Many of those who called for Jesus' crucifixion would soon discover God is more than willing to forgive our past, no matter what. No sin is so despicable, no weakness is so glaring, but that God cannot give a man a new start in life. And if God can forgive those who crucified His Son, you know He can forgive anything! For us, as for the people of Jerusalem, our God is more than willing to take our failures, our ignorance, and our mistakes, and work them back into His plan. If you don't give up on God, I can assure you, He will never give up on you.

The Bible says, "All things work for good to those who love God, who are called according to His purpose," and yes, that includes the crucifixion of our Lord. By His death on the cross, Jesus made possible our eternal life. When Jesus said, "It is finished," and breathed His last, the curtain in the Temple isolating the Holy of Holies from public view, was torn from top to bottom. God's presence was now available to all.

And what God did for them, yes, even for those who days before had called for the crucifixion of His son, He would like to do for you and me. We can agonize over past failures, surrender to our weaknesses, and cloud our days with self-pity. Or we can come to God, invite His forgiveness, and trust Him to lead us and make the days ahead the best days of our lives! It's never too late to become what you might have been!

– 11 –

Too Hot to Handle
On Temptation and Sin

Each one is tempted when, by his own evil desire, he is dragged away and enticed. Then, after desire has conceived, it gives birth to sin; and sin, when it is full-grown, gives birth to death.

James 1:14-15

IT WAS EARLY ONE Michigan morning when, in a rest area along I-94, a car pulled up in front of my Freightliner and came to a quick stop. I was on my way to Detroit with a load of cargo, and following a good night's sleep, had already gone through my morning routine. The coffee was made and safely placed in its holder on my dash, and I was ready to roll.

A young lady, perhaps in her mid-twenties, approached my truck. Attractive and looking as fresh as the morning dew, she smiled and asked, "Good morning, driver. Would you like to talk?"

"And what," I asked, "would you like to talk about?"

"Oh," she said, "I don't care. I'm just trying to pick up a little gas money."

It was then I realized that "talking" was not what she had in mind. "No, I don't think so," I responded.

"Are you sure?" she asked. "I won't tell if you won't."

"Sorry, lady, I don't believe so."

And then it was over. As she drove away, I realized that in just a matter of minutes, with a simple "yes" instead of a "no," I could have changed the direction of my life. I could have exposed myself to one of the social diseases, and it would have damaged my self-respect forever. That, however, would have been as nothing compared to the devastating impact it would have had on my relationship with God.

Like so much of what life has to offer, the big lie was that I could indulge in sin, and no one would ever know. At first glance, it would seem there would be no immediate cost (except for the $100 she would have charged) and no apparent penalty. Tempting? Absolutely! But sin is like that. It sneaks up on us when we least expect it.

And the battle with temptation and sin, even if successfully waged for a lifetime, will remain a threat until God calls me home. The moment I committed my life to model the Master, I challenged the forces of hell. And there will be no let-up. The devil is going to keep attacking my relationship with God through to the last moments of my life.

One would think, after serving the Lord for a lifetime, the pressures would ease. That, unfortunately, has not been the case. My battle with hell is as intense now as it was seventy years ago. Sin is always a threat, always an option; the devil will never give up.

I. Our Sinful Nature

The stark reality is that the predisposition to sin has been with us from our earliest days. Passed down to us from our forebearers, going back to Adam and Eve, it's in our genes. Whenever there is a conflict of interest, we always prefer to do our will as opposed to God's will. And *that*, the Bible says, is sin.

Life and reality have conditioned most of us to focus on specific temptations to sin, areas of susceptibility consistent with our predispositions. "The acts of our sinful nature," according to the Apostle Paul, "are obvious: sexual immorality, impurity, and debauchery; idolatry and witchcraft; hatred, discord, jealousy, fits of rage, selfish ambition, dissensions, factions, and envy; drunkenness, orgies, and the like" (Gal. 5:19-21).

These *sins*, and the list is far from complete, characterize many of those who live a life apart from God. We might look at the list and congratulate ourselves. Not guilty! But that is to miss the point. Our problem is not with *sins* but with *sin*, and *that* is another matter altogether. We are destroyed by our *sins*, but the culprit is our attraction to *sin*, defined as rebellion against the known will of God.

The Making of a Model

> Live by the Spirit, and you will not gratify the desires of the sinful nature. For the sinful nature desires what is contrary to the Spirit, and the Spirit what is contrary to the sinful nature (Gal. 5:16-17).

My tendency to sin, which is triggered by self-will, arrogance, and pride, will be with me as long as I live. If I am to achieve victory over the ungodly things I am tempted to *do*, I must first deal with what I *am*! When it comes to a life of holiness, *I* am my own worst enemy!

Self, as in self-image, self-centeredness, and self-ambition, has been and continues to be a monumental problem. I have my own weaknesses to fight and, despite a lifetime of serving the Lord, I continue to struggle. And there never seems to be a let-up. My drive to be the best I can be, my desire to model the Master, and my pursuit of God have been challenged in every way possible. I am engaged in a war with the forces of hell.

During my trip through my own "valley of the shadow of death" (Ps. 23:4), I spent twenty years struggling to make sense of what was happening to me. The loss of my stature as a minister of the Gospel, alienation from my family, and the absence of a meaningful reason for living was a nightmare so intense I find it difficult even now to reconstruct.

There were times when circumstances offered me a detour from the road down which God allowed me to travel. The chance for a second marriage in the early days of my journey, the possibility of sex without obligation on several occasions, and even thoughts of suicide during my lowest days, were options available to me during my twenty years as a single adult. But I discovered, again as per the Psalmist, "I will fear no evil for you are with me" (Ps. 23:4). God knew where I was, what I was going through, and He was gently preparing me for what lay ahead.

If Adam and Eve had never violated God's will and their progeny had not followed their example, sin would not be a problem. We would enjoy perfect harmony with God, the leadership of the Holy Spirit would be our sure and constant guide, and Jesus would be glorified in all we do. Perfect husbands would be married to perfect wives who would bear perfect children! Hard to imagine!

But until Christ returns to earth, it isn't going to happen. Satan is at war with God. He has no interest in us but has chosen to attack, and destroy if he can, our Father's most cherished creation: you and me.

II. The Satanic Agenda

If my understanding of Isaiah 14:12-15 is correct, Satan was "the morning star, son of the dawn," a unique creation of God, whose rebellion against God had its source in his pride.

> How you have fallen from heaven, O morning star.... You said in your heart, ... I will ascend above the tops of the clouds; I will make myself like the Most High.

It was pride that prompted Satan to challenge the sovereignty of God, and it is pride that drives him to threaten everything God has done for us. In 1 John 2:16, describing the world as Satan's domain, John gives us an insight into hell's strategy.

> For all that is in the world, the lust of the flesh, the lust of the eyes, and the pride of life, is not of the Father, but is of the world (KJV).

John was correct. Satan's strategy, initiated in the Garden of Eden, has never changed. He succeeded with Adam and Eve, tried the same tactic but failed with our Lord, and you can believe he will use a similar approach in his attempt to destroy you and me.

A. The Garden of Eden

Satan seldom reveals himself in a dramatic or extraordinary way. His approach is subtle and often unrecognized. When we least expect him, he takes us by surprise. And usually at our most vulnerable moment.

The devil never counterfeits dime-store jewelry. The girl that approached my truck that Michigan morning was attractive and appealing. She came across as warm, likable, and sweet. One could never have guessed that she was, in fact, an emissary from hell.

Analyze almost any temptation, and you will find it appeals to one or more of the fundamental characteristics of our nature. Pride, lust, and self-will are personality traits to which we are all susceptible.

We see this scenario played out for the first time in the Garden of Eden. Although in a different sequence from the order we have in 1 John 2:16, the principles are the same. Satan began with the *pride of life*.

I can imagine Satan joining Adam and Eve for a quiet lunch and a friendly conversation as among friends. I can't imagine a talking serpent, but perhaps, like the little green gecko of advertising fame, he came across as innocent and unassuming and took them completely by surprise. Indeed, his approach was so effective he has been using it ever since. He began by questioning God.

"Did God really say, 'You must not eat?' ... You will not surely die" (Gen. 3:1, 4).

It is telling that the very first temptation Adam and Eve faced in the Garden was to believe God did not really mean what He said, and the tendency to rationalize the clear word of God has been typical of mankind ever since. Inevitably, sin and deception soon follow.

It was an attractive offer, and Eve was hopeful. "God knows," Satan told her, "that when you eat [of the tree of the knowledge of good and evil] your eyes will be opened, and you will be like God, knowing good and evil" (Gen. 3:5). To be like God? That would be wonderful!

Then Satan aroused the *lust of the flesh* in Eve, again as per 1 John 2:16, when "the woman saw that it was good for food" (Gen. 3:6). As given to us repeatedly in the Apostle Paul's writings, the temptation to satisfy our instinctive self-interests, our drives, is something we all find appealing. "I can't believe one little bite will hurt," she must have thought. "And I *am* hungry!"

And then, finally, Satan stimulated the *lust of the eyes* when she saw the fruit was "pleasing to the eye" (Gen. 3:6). Surely something that looked that great couldn't be that bad! And as is true in much of life, it is true of sin: the dream is always more exciting than reality.

And the tactic Satan used, questioning God's clear mandate, is one he has used ever since. Trust in the word of God has been under threat from the earliest days of human history. Ours is a life of faith, and there will inevitably come a time when we must take God at His word and accept what He has told us without question.

It now becomes clear why our discussion in Chapter 9 on the authority of the Scriptures is critical to our study on *The Making of a Model*. The difficulty we sometimes have in taking God at His Word dates back to the Garden of Eden. "Did God really say *that*?" is a question that remains with us still.

The question Eve faced was personal rather than academic, but it raises an issue every generation of believers must address. If the devil can't get us to question the existence of God, if he can't get us to reject the deity of our Lord, he will challenge us by questioning the truthfulness of God's Word.

Again, I want to state my conviction that the Bible is true in whatever terms it speaks, including ethics, history, and science. I don't have all the answers to objections raised challenging the truth of God's Word. I refuse, however, to join Adam and Eve in questioning what God has said!

> All scripture is God-breathed and is useful for teaching, rebuking, correcting and training in righteousness, so that

the man of God may be thoroughly equipped for every good work (2 Tim. 3:16-17).

In simple terms, God said it, and I believe it.

B. The Wilderness of Judea

So successful had he been in the Garden of Eden, the devil made another attempt to thwart the divine will, this time in the wilderness of Judea. Again, he would question God's Word; again, he would give the subject of his attack an appealing alternative to the divine will. But the Son of Man, the Second Adam, wasn't interested; this time things would not go as the devil had hoped.

I am postulating that what we have in Matthew 4:1-11 is a condensed version of Jesus' encounter with Satan. I imagine there is much more to the conversation than the one recorded, and I wonder if it was so casual and unassuming it might have taken Jesus by surprise.

It was, perhaps, in the cool of the morning, with Jesus just awakening and hungry beyond belief, that a well-dressed traveler ambled by on a well-decked-out camel, acting as if surprised to find Jesus resting in the shade. Resplendent in all his finery, radiating promise and power, I can visualize him approaching an emaciated Jesus, catching Him, as he does all of us, at His weakest point. After a few minutes of friendly conversation, always willing to take his time if he can prompt a man's fall, I imagine him to have said,

> You know, Jesus, I just figured out who you are [Satan is lying through his teeth, but that, of course, is typical]. You're from Nazareth, aren't you? You are the one John baptized

about six weeks ago, the one he called 'the lamb of God, who takes away the sin of the world' (John 1:29). And you've been out here since then? With no food or anything to drink? Wow! Come on, man; this doesn't make a bit of sense. God doesn't work that way.

Listen ... *if* you are the Son of God, [in other words, if you're sure this whole business is for real], I think you should turn these stones into bread. You've sacrificed enough; as weak as you are, you deserve a good breakfast! Imagine these stones glowing like a freshly baked loaf of bread just out of the oven! Surely God doesn't want you to starve to death, so I can't imagine He will give you a bad time. Come on, man, use some common sense; you've got to have something to eat! Show me you really are the Son of God and do something! Here, turn this stone into bread!

The demands of Jesus' human nature, only to be expected in light of His lengthy fast, now become a temptation to sin. There was nothing unusual about Jesus' hunger nor anything inherently wrong in converting one of the stones into bread. But it wasn't in God's timing, and it wasn't God's way.

But there is much more happening here than at first meets the eye.

Jesus was fully God and fully man. It was necessary for Him to be divine, and therefore sinless if His sacrifice was to be acceptable to the Father. And, if He was to be a valid substitute by assuming the penalty of sin in our place, it was essential He do so as a man.

> [He] made himself of no reputation, and took upon him the form of a servant, and was made in the likeness of men (Phil. 2:7, KJV).

What Satan was inviting Jesus to do was to step outside His role as a man and exercise the power that was rightly His as God. But that was not the role the Father had determined for Him during His sojourn on earth. Such a move would have destroyed the divine plan and violated His role as a typical human being.

But Jesus was not about to accept Satan's invitation, no matter how hungry He must have been. The temptation was genuine. Jesus *was* desperately hungry, and He was surely too weak to walk the nearly one hundred miles to Capernaum when this wilderness experience was all over.

But Jesus was under divine mandate, and He was not interested in doing anything that could be misrepresented or misunderstood. "Man does not live on bread alone," Jesus responded, quoting Deut. 8:3, "but on every word that comes from the mouth of God" (Matt. 4:11). There was no way Jesus was going to use God's power to satisfy a personal need.

It is telling that, as in the Garden of Eden, the first temptation revolved around a natural, understandable human need. The temptations to follow were far more sinister. But Satan, never one to give up easily, chose a fresh approach: he challenged Jesus' pride.

He took Jesus, and we aren't told how, to the highest point of the temple. "*If you are the Son of God,*" he said, "prove it! Throw yourself down. The Bible says, 'He will command his angels concerning you ... so that you will not strike your foot against a stone,' (Psa. 91:11-12). "Go ahead; you'll be ok."

"Absolutely not!" Jesus responded, quoting Deut. 6:26. "Do not tempt the Lord your God." Satan had been foiled again!

Not yet ready to give up the devil then turned to what 1 John 2:16 calls *the lust of the eyes*.

He took Jesus to a "very high mountain" to show Him "all the kingdoms of the world" (Matt. 4:8). Again, we are not told how Satan got this accomplished, but it is clear from the record the temptation was genuine. *All* humanity could be saved; universal salvation without the cross.

To quote the *Message* version of the New Testament,

> The devil took him to the peak of a huge mountain. He gestured expansively, pointing out all the earth's kingdoms, how glorious they all were. Then he said, "They're all yours—lock, stock, and barrel. Just go down on your knees and worship me, and they're yours" (Matt. 4:8-9).

I can't believe Satan was ignorant enough to think Jesus would buy the argument, but it *was* an impressive offer. Jesus, the devil implied, would be allowed to offer universal salvation without a cross and manifest His glory without opposition. But there was a catch: He had to worship the devil!

Jesus finally decided it was time to quit the charade. Satan had nothing to offer, but it sounded good, and the temptations were real. But Jesus had had enough! "Bug off, Mister! It is written, 'Worship the Lord your God and serve him only'" (Matt. 4:10).

Satan had met his match, and Jesus was not about to be dissuaded from His mission. They would meet again and again, and then, in final combat, they would face off at the cross. It would be the devil's ultimate moment of ecstasy, and for six hours, all hell would be having a party.

But then, reverberating through the darkness, there would be heard the cry of the victor. "It is finished!" (John 19:30). Salvation by the works of the law, finished! The threat of death, finished! Sin's hold on humanity, finished! The Son's separation from the Father, finished! Thank God Almighty, it was finished, finished at last!

I have been writing about *The Making of a Model*.

The process that leads to modeling success is meant to bring us, as it did for Jesus, to a Jordan river experience where we are filled with the Holy Spirit and hear the voice of God. But the ecstasy is always short-lived, for inevitably, the road from the Jordan leads into the wilderness!

I understand the implications of the temptation and fall in the Garden of Eden, but it is in the temptation of Jesus that I find a truth that speaks to me in my endeavor to model the Master. Again I am reminded that we should never be surprised when our most cherished moments with God take us into a wilderness of our own. If we are going to model the Master, we must expect that we, too, will find that an attack from hell will almost certainly follow every high moment with God.

The devil had to give up on Jesus, for a short time at least, and within days, Jesus was back in Galilee. But the devil was not about to give up, and he would dog Jesus' footsteps through the next three years of Jesus' ministry until, finally, with Jesus on the cross, he would think himself the victor.

But Satan did not win that fight, and he need not win with you and me.

Some years ago, mid-day as I recall, at a truck stop in Birmingham, Alabama, I had an attractive twenty-something knock on my truck door and ask if she could use my CB radio for just a moment. I was new to the trucking industry and very naïve, and I said, "Ok. Come on up."

She took her place in the driver's seat, turned on my radio, and said, "Good morning, guys. Would any of you like some company? I'm commercial ... and I can guarantee you will not be disappointed."

It was a set-up. She was hoping, now that she was in my truck, I would suggest she spend some time with *me*. And no one would ever know; it all seemed so easy.

That I was not interested was not a problem for another trucker promptly took her up on the offer. She moved on and within minutes I was back on the road, wiser but no worse for the experience. But the temptation was there, proposing compromise without accountability, pleasure without penalty, and evil without consequence.

"Be self-controlled and alert," writes the Apostle Peter. "Your enemy the devil prowls around like a roaring lion looking for someone to devour." But then he adds this promise, "And the God of all grace, who called you to his eternal glory in Christ, after you have suffered a little while, will himself restore you and make you strong, firm and steadfast" (1 Pet. 5:8, 10). The devil is real, and he never gives up. He will challenge everything we believe, distort every truth, magnify every mistake, and intensify every conflict. He will, in short, exploit every opportunity we give him. Modeling the Master will never go unchallenged!

You and I are caught in the crosshairs of a royal war, but we are on the winning side. Satan may not yet be prepared to face reality, but he is a defeated foe.

> Yea, doubtless, we are more than conquerors through Him who loved us. For I am convinced that neither death nor life, neither angels nor demons ... nor anything else in all creation, will be able to separate us from the love of God that is in Christ Jesus our Lord (Rom. 8:37-39).

Blessed by the Name of the Lord!

– Strategies for Living #8 –
A Sin-City Vacation

I was sitting next to a fifty-something in a Las Vegas Casino, and we were discussing our visit to Las Vegas, popularly known as Sin City. I was a long-haul trucker in town on business, he a vacationing British tourist.

Before I finished my first cup of coffee, and without any prompting, the gentleman, whom I will call Nick, interrupted my thoughts.

"I can't believe how easy it is to get a girl in this city, and man, compared to Great Britain, they're cheap. Haven't decided yet… but I may get another one tonight. I'm not married so it's no big deal … I'll see how I feel this evening."

But it *was* a big deal; he just didn't know it. I can't say I was shocked, but I *was* impressed by his candor and willingness to discuss his promiscuous lifestyle. It was, I thought, remarkable that Nick was pleased to discuss his pleasures with a complete stranger, unaware of what his choices said about his character and moral responsibility.

It never occurred me until later that Nick may have been pimping in hopes of a discount. Regardless, Nick was pleased with his visit. In his world, these "girls" were perfect. They were willing, for a price, to give him pleasure without penalty, intimacy without emotional involvement, a liaison without consequence. It promised to be a week he would never forget.

Let us presume for the sake of argument that he was not infected by an std, that no irate boyfriend threatened his life, that no unwanted pregnancy ensued. It is more than likely that, except for the loss of several hundred dollars, his visit to Las Vegas was of no consequence, little more than a break in the routine.

Sin is like that. Eliminate God from the picture, maintain that all truth is relative, conclude that there is no such thing as objective right and wrong, and you're free to live as you please. And it works. If sin wasn't so much fun, it wouldn't be so popular. It is little wonder many people see no need for God. They are doing just fine without Him, thank you very much!

But there *is* a problem. "What you sow, that you will also reap" (Gal. 6:7). And then there is the matter of life after death. In light of his lifestyle, it is likely Nick believed, or at least hoped, that death ends it all. That may be a convenient out, but it is not supported by either Jesus or the New Testament writers. "Man is destined to die once," the Bible says, "but after that to face judgment.

You will hear one of these days that, "Scott has passed away." But don't you believe it! I've moved; I've gone home. In the words of the Apostle Paul, "There is laid up for me a crown of righteousness, which the Lord ... shall give me at that day."

There is a heaven in my future... and I can hardly wait!

– 12 –

Seeing the Invisible
Faith Amid the Storm

This is the assurance we have in approaching God: that if we ask anything according to his will, he hears us. And if we know that he hears us – whatever we ask – we know that we have what we asked of him.

1 John 5:14-15

WHEN NOAH EMERGED from the ark to a pristine, renewed world, little did he realize the tremendous responsibility God was about to place on him and his family.

> Then God blessed Noah and his sons, saying to them, "Be fruitful and increase in number and fill the earth. The fear and dread of you will fall upon all the beasts of the earth ... they are given into your hands. Everything that lives and moves will be food for you. Just as I gave you the green plants, I now give you everything" (Gen. 9:1-3).

The Making of a Model

The premise of *The Making of a Model* is that Jesus has commissioned you and me to serve as His royal representatives on earth. Were it not for the fact we serve a God who majors on the impossible that call would be little more than an empty dream. But God has granted us the privilege to approach Him through the medium of prayer. And it is in the place of prayer we discover the God of the miraculous. We *can* model the Master!

In John 14:12-14, Jesus said,

> I tell you the truth, anyone who has faith in me will do what I have been doing. He will do even greater things than these because I am going to the Father. And I will do whatever you ask in my name, so that the Son may bring glory to the Father. You may ask me for anything in my name, and I will do it.

I believe Jesus meant what He said. This promise has prompted Jesus' followers to come to Him boldly for personal needs, for strength during times of stress, and, yes, as per the theme of this work, that we might become effective living models of the Master Himself.

Following Dr. Billy Graham's death on Feb 21, 2018, Christians around the world, many of whom had been converted under his ministry, celebrated his life.

But there is much to Billy Graham's story most people know little about. His son Franklin, in an article entitled *Prayer for Revival, 80 Years Ago*, makes a special point.

> Eighty years ago this month, a group of businessmen gathered under a grove of shade trees at the edge of a

pasture for a prayer meeting. They had met several times before at different locations around their hometown of Charlotte, NC—always outdoors—to pray for revival in their city, revival across their state, and revival to the ends of the earth. ...

W. Franklin Graham [Billy Graham's father] was part of the prayer group, and on this occasion in May 1934, he hosted the gathering on his dairy farm. That day a paper salesman named Vernon Patterson suggested they add a bold new prayer, that God would raise up someone from Charlotte who would take the Gospel to the ends of the earth. ... Billy Graham, who was only 15 years old, was at that moment in the barn doing his after-school chores. ...

None of those who prayed were thinking of young Billy, who had not yet given his heart to Jesus Christ as Lord and Savior. And my father, pitching hay to the mules, was daydreaming about a career as a professional baseball player.

Not a one of the men present, including Billy's father, realized what a remarkable ministry that fifteen-year-old boy-in-the-barn would someday have in answer to that prayer. But Billy Graham, in due time, preached to more people, in more countries, than any other man in history.

And it all began with a group of men who took time to pray!

I. When Jesus Prayed

It was on the way to the Garden of Gethsemane, perhaps when passing through a vineyard, that Jesus was prompted to comment on the vine and the branches as recorded in John 15. Before moving to the Garden, Jesus paused to utter the most sublime prayer ever recorded. The Son of God, facing the greatest crisis of His life, prayed first for His disciples, and by extension, for you and me.

Within a few minutes He would move to the Garden of Gethsemane and have a final, intimate conversation with His Father. He would soon be devastated by everything hell could throw at Him. In the Garden, He would pray for Himself.

But that was not His focus here. At this point He had but one thought: the Father's glory by, in, and through His disciples and the church.

A. Jesus Prayed that the Father might be Glorified

> Father ... Glorify your Son, that your Son may glorify you. ... Father, glorify me in your presence with the glory I had with you before the world began. ... I am not praying for the world, but for those you have given me, for they are yours. ... Holy Father, protect them by the power of your name — the name you gave me — so that they may be one as we are one. ... Sanctify them by the truth; your word is truth (John 17:1, 5, 9, 11, 17).

Twice, in both vs. 1 and vs. 5, Jesus asks that *He* might be glorified.

Jesus' attitude, as seen in verse 1, highlights a principle we must take to heart. If we are to glorify the Father it will happen only to the extent that we magnify Jesus Himself. "I tell you the truth," Jesus said, "anyone who has faith in me will do what I have been doing. ... And I will do whatever you ask in my name *so that the Son may bring glory to the Father*" (John 14: 12, 13).

If we are to serve as living models of Jesus Christ, we must understand the driving force in Jesus' life. Jesus first prayed for his own glorification, but with one overriding objective: that the *Father* might be glorified.

That was Jesus' mission. And it was the mission He was about to leave in the hands of His disciples. He knew what was at stake. They were, by human standards, only a small group of uneducated, hard-working, salt-of-the-earth men. But for the fact they had been with Jesus and would soon be filled with God's Holy Spirit, they would have quickly faded from history. Soon, however, they were going to "turn the world upside down" (Acts. 17:6, KJV).

Jesus was about to encounter the most difficult period of His life. He knew what is at stake, and how much of what He came to earth to accomplish was going to depend on their insight, courage, and faithfulness.

Accordingly, then, before He prays for Himself, Jesus prays for His disciples.

B. Jesus Prayed that the Disciples might be Sanctified

> My prayer is not that you take them out of the world but that you protect them from the evil one. They are not of the world, even as I am not of it. Sanctify them by the truth; your word is truth (John 17:15-17).

Sanctification, that act of God whereby He sets apart a person, place or thing that His purposes may be accomplished, describes a life in tune and in harmony with God.

Significantly, Jesus did not pray that His disciples be removed from the world or shielded from the challenges of life. They would need wisdom and faith and courage, but that was not His focus here. His immediate concern was for their protection from the evil one *and* their sanctification.

Jesus' disciples would soon be devastated by their Masters' crucifixion, and hell would convince them, for a few days at least, that the battle was over. Jesus had done His best to prepare them for the inevitable, but He knew they were not ready.

Their three-year journey with Jesus was about to end. The forces of hell, which had concentrated on Jesus and His mission, would soon be turned on them. "Satan has asked to sift all of you as wheat," Jesus told Peter, "but I have prayed for you, Simon, that your faith may not fail" (Luke. 22:31-32).

"Not so," Peter responded, "I'm ready to go with you to the death" (Luke 22:33). But he was to learn the devil is real and must be taken seriously. "Your enemy the devil," he would later write, "prowls around like a roaring lion looking for someone to devour. Resist him, standing firm in the faith" (1 Pet. 5:8-9).

Peter's greatest problem, he would soon learn, was not the devil; the devil he could resist. Peter's greatest problem was Peter. And likewise, I identify with the Apostle, for I find that for me, too, I am my own greatest enemy.

I need God, and there is reason prayer has, for me, become the cornerstone of my Christian life. If I am to model the Master, if I am to measure up to His call on my life, I need His intervention. Indeed, what I need from God is tantamount to a miracle!

II. When I Pray

Prayer is based on a relationship, a relationship I believe essential if I am to become a living model of Jesus Christ. He *must* become the driving force in my life.

God is not a puppet on a string, and He doesn't bounce to my call. God, however, has intervened in my life on several occasions and I have recounted some of these events in this work. Seldom, however, have I had an objective, direct, provable answer to prayer.

I have never heard a voice or had a vision, and I question most impressions that flit through my mind. It is amazing, however, as I look at my life over an extended period of time, how events have coalesced to bring about significant change. I do not expect instant gratification; that would constitute a miracle. But God does answer prayer, every prayer, and He does so most generally through normal means. He is the Master Strategist of the universe, working with people and circumstances to bring about the fulfillment of His will. I know ... sometimes it seems that God is sooooooo slow! But it often takes time for all the pieces to fall into place, and God never rushes.

The Scriptures, however, tell us clearly that we serve a prayer-answering God. I believe my present station in life, as a case in point, is a direct answer to prayer. The despair and trauma of those early days following the break-up of our marriage make my present status border on the miraculous. Friends prayed ... we prayed ... and God gave us the wisdom to put our marriage back together and discover once again a place of service in the Kingdom of God.

God, then, does answer prayer.

A. When Our Requests are Denied

When He does not, however, there are five factors that may indicate why God has been unwilling, or unable, to move on our behalf.

1. The sin factor

It is possible that sin, defined here as the willful disregard of God's known will, may, in fact, have *prevented* God from doing the very thing He would like to do in and through our lives.

> Surely the arm of the Lord is not too short to save, nor his ear too dull to hear. But your iniquities have separated you from your God; your sins have hidden his face from you so that he will not hear (Isa. 59:1-2).

Believing prayer, faith, is based on a life that is in a right relationship with God. We live in a society so perverted by sin we may look like saints by comparison, but God does not grade on a curve. If we are looking to Him for divine intervention, it is essential that we honor Him in every area of our lives. Prayer, as already stated, is not an activity; it is a relationship.

"Dear friends," writes the Apostle John, "if our heart do not condemn us, we have confidence before God and receive from him anything we ask, because we obey his commands and do what pleases him" (1 John 3:21-23).

2. The lust factor

After a lifetime of serving the Lord, you would think I could rest on my laurels. That, however, has not been the case. The attractiveness of sin, the temptation to compromise the standards of holiness God has ordained, is as threatening as it was seventy years ago. I know better, and I am better able to address the lies hell keeps dishing out. But at no time am I free from new challenges to the will of God for my life.

Lust, better known as *sins of the flesh,* are, I believe, our greatest obstacle in the exercise of faith and believing prayer. In the words of James, the brother of our Lord,

> But every man is tempted, when he is drawn away of his own lust, and enticed. Then when lust hath conceived, it bringeth forth sin: and sin, when it is finished, bringeth forth death (Jas. 1:14-15, KJV).

And it is not just our moral tendencies that are in view here. Even though we may have our hormones under control, pride, temper, and the desire to do as we please can devastate our walk with God. Even though these tendencies are what one would expect since we are human, they cannot be easily dismissed.

We march to the beat of a different drummer. We are called to model the Master, and there comes a point in each of our lives when we must make a hard decision: are we going to *model the Master* or are we not? No excuses, no detours, and without compromise ... are we, or are we not, prepared to walk in the footsteps of the Master?

That, for me, has been an awesomely difficult decision. There is no way the devil is going to allow me to proceed without doing everything possible to get me off-track. God, however, has given me a solution. "Live by the Spirit, and you will not gratify the desires of the sinful nature" (Gal. 5:16). That is God's way.

As I will indicate in the chapter to follow, the longer I serve the Lord, the greater has been my dependence on the work of the Spirit in my life. The call to model the Master is a great objective, but I have found it impossible to serve as one of God's living models apart from the presence and power of His Holy Spirit.

3. The freedom factor

There is no draft in the Kingdom of God; all of us are volunteers.

I have family for whom I have prayed every day for the last fifteen years. They are still far from God, and while I respect their independence and self-serving ways, I continue to pray for them. If there was anything I could do that would guarantee their commitment to Christ, I would do so. The freedom of choice, however, is a facet of our human nature God Himself will never violate.

> When I say to the wicked, 'O wicked man, you will surely die,' and you do not speak out to dissuade him from his ways, that wicked man will die for his sin, and I will hold you accountable for his blood. But if you do warn the wicked

man to turn from his ways and he does not do so, he will die for his sin, but you will have saved yourself" (Ezek. 33:8-9).

Again we are reminded how critical it is we model the Master wherever we are and whatever the circumstances of our life. We represent the Master, and the imprint of Jesus on our lives is something you can be sure the Holy Spirit will use to speak to their hearts.

God's people are always on display. We may be limited in what we can *say,* and others may challenge what we *believe,* but those who know us best can't argue with who we *are.*

4. The Denial Factor

There are times when, having come to God for help regarding a special need, God simply says, "No!" Ours is a walk of faith, and there are times when we must trust that God is doing or allowing that which He knows is best for us.

The Apostle Paul is a classic case in point.

Dogged throughout his lifetime with an ailment which I believe was a problem with his eyes, God's answer to the Apostle's prayer was a flat denial.

In his own words,

> To keep me from becoming conceited, because of these surpassingly great revelations, there was given me a thorn in the flesh. ... Three times I pleaded with the Lord to take it away from me. But he said, "My grace is sufficient for you, for my power is made perfect in weakness" (2 Cor. 12:7-9).

Our God is not a puppet on a string, and He does not react every time we cry for release. It's not that God doesn't care. But we are part of the human family, and serving the Lord is no cop-out from the pressures of life that are common to us all.

If we are to model the Master, we do our modeling not only when the sun is shining. Life is not all peaches and cream, and it has a way of sometimes overwhelming us with unbelievable stress. Indeed, there are times when our most powerful modeling is done during times of crisis and pain. And then we too, along with the Apostle, can testify that His "grace is sufficient," that His power "is made perfect in weakness."

5. The Delay Factor

We must always trust God to do what He knows is best. God's delay is not always God's denial. In Luke 18, Jesus spoke of the insistent widow and then applied this truth: persistence in prayer may, indeed, move the hand of God.

Until we hear from God, it is perfectly proper that we continue to bring our issues before Him. Even, however, when we are in tune with God and convinced we have prayed according to His will, there will be times when must hold steady and trust God to do what He knows best.

If we were to think of our life as a giant puzzle, an image patterned after Jesus Christ, it is not hard to see it may take time before all the pieces fit together. We are, however, in the hands of a loving God, and if we cooperate with the design He has devised for our life, in the end, we can be assured: we *will* model the Master.

B. When We Can Pray with Faith

God promises to answer all prayer that is consistent with His will.

> This is the assurance we have in approaching God: that if we ask anything according to his will, he hears us. And if we know that he hears us. And if we know that he hears us — whatever we ask — we know that we have what we asked of him (1 John 5:14-15).

Even then, however, it is true that God doesn't always work as quickly or in just the way we think He should. We want instant satisfaction, a miraculous intervention, but God, more often than not, works through a process. That takes time and it is imperative that we trust Him to do what He knows best.

1. We can pray for forgiveness when we have sinned

"When you pray, say: ... Forgive us our sins" (Luke 11:2, 4).

Although I can claim few direct, objective, provable answers to prayer, I *have* had a brush with the miraculous. The dramatic change that comes to a person's life when they have invited Jesus Christ to be the Lord of their lives is, hands down, the greatest miracle I have ever seen in answer to prayer.

I remember the Sunday morning a lady I shall call Janet came forward in a public profession of faith and invited Jesus Christ to become the Lord of her life.

I had preached a simple message that Sunday morning, but for Janet, it was a moment of truth. In the process of preaching, I had said something like, "God wants to do a work in your life." Then, as I often did in preaching, I reached out with my index finger, pointing toward the audience to emphasize the point. Janet later told me that when she looked up, I was pointing right at her. God, she later told me, spoke to her heart, and within minutes she came forward and gave me the awesome privilege of praying with her.

A miracle of divine grace took place that day in Janet's life. Muscular dystrophy had devastated her body, but God performed a miracle in her spirit. It took only one prayer and only one moment in time, but Janet became a "new creation" in Jesus Christ. Prayer works!

2. We can pray to be strengthened by the Holy Spirit

> I pray that out of his glorious riches he may strengthen you with power through his Spirit in your inner being (Eph. 3:16).

In my quest to serve as a living model of Jesus Christ, I have had to face the fact that there is no way I can achieve the Christlikeness for which I have spent a lifetime praying without the active work of the Holy Spirit in my life.

> Jesus said, "If you then, being evil, know how to give good gifts unto your children: how much more shall your heavenly Father give the Holy Spirit to them that ask him? (Luke 11:13).

Were it not for the empowering presence of God's Spirit, I would despair of ever reaching the level of maturity I believe to be God's will for my life. In my battle against sin, the flesh, and the devil, I discover I am my own greatest enemy. There is no way I can measure up to the challenges before me without divine help. But I remain confident of ultimate victory, for I have this assurance, as stated by the Apostle Paul, "Live by the Spirit, and you will not gratify the desires of the sinful nature" (Gal. 5:16).

3. We can pray for wisdom

The Christian is called to model the Master in a society that, frankly, doesn't want to hear it. We are fighting against the current, living among people who will challenge everything we believe.

"If any of you lacks wisdom," wrote James, the brother of our Lord, "he should ask God, who gives generously (Jas. 1:5).

We are marching to the beat of a different drummer, and God is more than able to give us the leadership we need that He might be glorified in all we do.

4. We can pray for divine healing

Again, from James, "Therefore, confess your sins to each other and pray for each other so that you may be healed (Jas. 5:16).

My faith in God's power to heal comes close to home.

As my father stepped from his second-floor office in our home one morning in 1949, he could scarcely believe what he was seeing on the floor twelve feet below. Lying face down, bleeding from the left ear, and unconscious, he saw what was left of me following a fall that came perilously close to ending my life.

The Making of a Model

The stairway that led to the ground floor of our home was sided by a winding, smooth banister that no self-respecting ten-year-old could ignore. The trick was to slide down the banister and reach the first floor in record time. This time I missed! How I survived I do not know but, surprisingly, my injuries were minimal. Despite a broken collarbone and reduced hearing in my left ear, I recovered completely within just a few months.

And now, the rest of the story.

My parents were missionaries, and, at the time of this incident, we were living in Cusco, Peru. A week or so later, my father received a letter from a lady in the United States he had, to the best of his knowledge, never met. "Could it be," she wrote, "that you had a particularly bad day on Wednesday? As I was working around my home, I felt a special burden to pray for you. I stopped what I was doing, prayed for you and your family until the burden lifted, and I write to let you know of my experience and ask how you and your family are doing."

My father wrote back, thanking her for her faithfulness, and never heard from her again. But that was the very day our family was in desperate need of divine intervention.

Some will say that my experience was just a fortunate coincidence. It is amazing, however, how often such *coincidences* follow a request made to our Heavenly Father. God answers prayer. Our Father is a Master Strategist, and He has an uncanny way of controlling events whereby all the pieces fall into place at just the right time! Skeptics may call it circumstantial; we call it God.

From Jesus own lips, this promise:

> I tell you the truth, anyone who has faith in me will do what I have been doing. He will do even greater things than these because I am going to the Father. And I will do whatever you ask in my name, so that the Son may bring glory to the Father. You may ask me for anything in my name, and I will do it (John 14:12-14).

That is a powerful, all-inclusive promise given us by our Lord Himself. There is life-changing, eternally significant power in prayer.

In the summer of 2015, I traveled to Spokane, WA, for my mother's funeral. At 96 she was clearly tired of living and was not only prepared but anxious to finally go home to encounter the Lord she had followed for a lifetime.

While in Washington I decided to rent an auto and revisit old haunts. Poulsbo, just across the Puget Sound from Seattle, had been my home for many years. The decision to visit the city again and remember old times, see old friends, and revisit old haunts, was an unforgettable experience. I love the northwest and the seven years I lived in Poulsbo was a time that brings back only fond and cherished memories. Were it not for family, devoted New Englander's, all, I would be living there still.

While there I decided to visit Mt. Rainier, seen for years only from a great distance. When I got to the Visitor's Center

I was surprised to discover that the snow cap, even in midsummer, came right down to the parking lot.

As I laid a hand on the frigid ice I was impressed by the great mountain. The ice glistened in the morning sun from the parking lot to the mountain's 14,409 ft. peak, brilliantly outlined against a cloudless, deep blue sky. Mt. Rainier was magnificent.

The experience was something of a metaphor of my life.

I have faced many a mountain in my journey, and at first glance, each has seemed formidable and unyielding. Unbelievable challenges have often left me shaken and hurting.

There were times when I was so disoriented by stress and fear I could not pray; I had no clue how I was going to survive. Indeed, the despair was so intense and the trauma was so overwhelming, those days have been blocked out of my mind and are now beyond recall.

Here I am, however, years later, pleased to tell you that I struggled through the valley and fought my way up the mountain, and discovered that if you walk with God, sooner or later, you will break out into the sunshine of a new day!

Blessed be the name of the Lord!

– From My Daily Journal #4 –
In Pursuit of His Excellence

*Jesus withdrew with his disciples to the lake,
and a large crowd from Galilee followed. Mk. 3:7*

But you are a chosen people, a royal priesthood, a holy nation ... that you may declare the praises of him who called you out of darkness into his wonderful light. 1 Peter. 2:8

Pastor Josh, in a message on Mark 3:7-12, entitled, "When Jesus Withdraws," made the following observation, and I paraphrase:

Too many Christians want God to tell them what to do ... who to marry, where to go to school, when to brush their teeth, in short, to be in complete control of their lives. We note here, however, that Jesus withdrew from the crowd, beyond the reach of those who wanted healing and a touch from the Master. God, you see, doesn't want us to be puppets on a string. We were not designed to be slaves to an autocratic God. We, in this sense, are not sheep blindly following a God who tells us what to do and when to do it; we were created a kingdom of priests and God expects us to take responsibility for our lives.

What a profound thought! In my search to know and do the will of God, it has often been my temptation to sit back and do nothing until somehow prompted by God to move out of my comfortable lifestyle into a life of active service. Grant the point that too often I have gone off half-cocked into areas of activity that turned out to be counter-productive, but that is not the issue here.

God is not going to drive us to do something we are simply too lazy to accomplish. We note that all during Jesus' ministry, he slowly withdrew from the crowds. When He could have had the people of Israel "eating out of His hand," He withdrew from all except for a few selected ones to whom He appeared after the resurrection ... then He left them for good, placing them into the hands of the Holy Spirit.

There is surely a sense in which we need to wait on God for direction and wisdom ... but God has no interest in maintaining us as a puppet on a string, and I think this was Josh's point. We don't want to accept responsibility; we would, in fact, rather that God take the fall for whatever happens. It is, however, my life and my responsibility to be in tune, to live a life so very close to Him, that by nature and instinct, I live the life He would have me to live, doing those things that will honor Him. With an open heart and a sincere commitment to live His will, I can be assured that when God has something to say He will do so -- in that *quiet whisper* that is so characteristic of the way in which He directs my life.

Until then, however, it is imperative that I respond to the direction He has already given me and live my life in pursuit of His excellence ... taking advantage of every opportunity that comes my way ... to glorify Him.

PART FIVE

The Model Perfected

We are all pencils in the hand of a writing God, who is sending love letters to the world.

~ Mother Teresa ~

– 13 –

The Go-Between Spirit
Appropriating the Power of God

When he, the Spirit of truth, comes, he will guide you into all truth. He will not speak on his own; he will speak only what he hears, and he will tell you what is yet to come. He will bring glory to me by taking from what is mine and making it known to you.

John 16:13-14

MODELING THE MASTER has become, for many of us, life's greatest challenge. Human drives and ambitions, making a living, and rearing a family all call for our attention. The many voices directing our thinking toward prosperity and success in both the material and the spiritual realm often leave us confused and in need of divine direction.

The Making of a Model

Recognizing the challenges facing His disciples, Jesus told them,

> It is to your advantage that I go away; for if I do not go away, the Helper will not come to you; but if I go, I will send Him to you (John 16:7).

They had just spent three years with the most influential and outstanding Man the world has ever known. They had seen Him doing the inconceivable, watched Him overcome impossible odds, heard from Him truth more profound than anything the prophets had written. And now He tells them it is *good* He is about to leave?

There was no way the disciples could imagine what they would do in His absence, much less how it could be to their advantage. What, or rather, who, could replace Him? He had corrected their misunderstandings, arbitrated their conflicts, broadened their knowledge, and given them hope. Was his absence to be to their good? Unbelievable!

"But do not despair," if I may paraphrase, "I will not leave you alone. I am going to send you the Holy Spirit."

They had followed Jesus for three years and seen what *He* did under the direction and power of God's Spirit. But Jesus told them not to worry. They were about to experience the same presence and power they had seen operative in His life; they were about to host the presence of God in the Person of the Holy Spirit.

> Anyone who has faith in me will do what I have been doing. He will do even greater things than these, because I am going to the Father. ... And I will ask the Father and he will

13 – The Go-Between Spirit

give you another Counselor to be with you forever — the Spirit of truth (John 14:12, 16).

While the disciples knew Jesus on a surface level … His mannerisms, interests, looks, voice, etc. … they never knew Him on a personal level *until after the resurrection and the coming of the Holy Spirit.* They didn't "get it" until after Pentecost. Their five senses saw, heard, felt, touched, and, perhaps, even smelled Him, but not until Pentecost did their hearts and minds tune in to what He was all about.

Likewise, I will never experience Him in a life-altering way except by the power and activity of the Holy Spirit. This, I am convinced, is what the coming of the Holy Spirit into my life is all about.

I. The Point of Departure

I cannot imagine where I would be in my drive to model the Master were it not for the work of the Holy Spirit in my life. "When the Counselor comes," Jesus said, "he will testify about me" (John 15:26). That, for me, is what the Holy Spirit is all about.

From my earliest days, I dedicated my life to knowing everything I could about Jesus Christ. I was captivated by the facts of His life, the principles He taught, and the mandate He left. Far from being satisfied, however, I felt short-changed. Something was missing. What I wanted was to *know* Him, as did Paul, in "the power of his resurrection, and the fellowship of sharing in his sufferings, becoming like him in his death" (Phil 3:10).

The Making of a Model

It is difficult for me to realize that, along with every other believer, I have been called to become God's dwelling place on earth.

> Do you not know that your body is a temple of the Holy Spirit, who is in you, whom you have received from God? (1 Cor. 6:19)

I began my pursuit of God during my teen years. It has been a difficult journey. Despite an openness to the work of the Spirit, the drive to overcome sin and live a model life has not brought about the spiritual maturity I would have expected. I have feared demeaning the work of the Spirit in light of my own track record. I am a work in process.

But I have been strengthened by Jesus' promise. He stated that the Holy Spirit will "teach you all things and will remind you of everything I have said" (John 14:26). And in John 15:26, "the Spirit of truth who goes out from the Father, he will testify about me." And again, in John 16:13, "when He, the Spirit of truth comes, He will guide you into all truth. ... he will take what is mine and make it known to you."

Where would I be but for the work of the Holy Spirit?

Gordon Fee is right on when he writes,

> Pentecostals have often been accused of exegeting their own experience and then looking to the Bible to support it. In part this may be true, but it is important to know why they have done so. On the one hand, their experience itself has been so empowering, so thoroughly life-changing, both in terms of personal obedience to God and readiness and empowerment for witness, that they instinctively know that it must be of God—and therefore must be biblical (*Gospel and Spirit*, 107).

13 – The Go-Between Spirit

It is critical to the work of the Spirit in my life that there be no detours, no breaks in my relationship with God. And I write here not of outright sin, but such things as impatience, temper, impure thoughts, moments in which the presence of God is interrupted by my human predispositions. The books I read, the programs I watch, the things I talk about with friends must be carefully guarded that there be no interruptions, no time-outs in my fellowship with the Spirit.

In the words of the Apostle Paul,

> Do not quench the Spirit. ... May God himself, the God of peace, sanctify you through and through. May your whole spirit, soul and body be kept blameless at the coming of our Lord Jesus Christ (1 Thess. 5:19, 23).

If I propose to live under the leadership of the Holy Spirit, it is a commitment that must be upheld 24/7. In short, if I am to model the Master, I must *model the Master*! However difficult the situation, however distracting the problem, I must live in complete harmony and under the complete control of God's Holy Spirit.

From Romans 8:9, it is clear that, at the moment of conversion, the Holy Spirit comes into the life of every believer. "If anyone does not have the Spirit of Christ, they do not belong to Christ," we are told. And, again, in 1 Cor. 12:13, the Apostle writes, "For we were all baptized by one Spirit into one body — whether Jews or Gentiles, slave or free — and we were all given the one Spirit to drink."

Some time ago, in a Friday morning Bible study with a group of Christian gentlemen, the question was raised: when

The Making of a Model

did the disciples become Christians? Fortunately for us, Jesus did not leave us hanging on this one.

On the evening of Resurrection Sunday, Jesus met with His disciples. Thomas was absent, but to the other ten, He said, "As the Father has sent me, I am sending you." And then, to their surprise, He "breathed" on them and said, "Receive the Holy Spirit" (John 20:21-22).

> This experience was not simply a promise, an anticipation of the greater effusion to be poured out upon them at Pentecost. The word here translated "receive" cannot merely promise a reception belonging to the future but expresses a reception actually present (Ervin, *Spirit Baptism*, 17).

As happens at conversion for every believer, the Holy Spirit came into their lives. That was the moment they transitioned from being under the Old to be under the New Covenant. A new creation had taken place; they had just been born again!

When Jesus breathed on them, He breathed His life into them. For the previous three years, Jesus had been *with* them; He was now to be *in* them. This is what the Apostle Paul described in Col. 1:27 as, "Christ in you the hope of glory.

The essence of conversion is that the Holy Spirit has come into each of our lives, even though we were once dead in "transgressions and sins" (Eph. 2:1), and re-energized our dysfunctional spirit. Thus, we were endowed with the very presence of God. And thank God for it! Without His presence in our lives, there is no way anyone of us could hope to model the Master.

From the very first moment of my surrender to Jesus as a typical ten-year-old, the Spirit of God came into my life and "testified with my spirit that I was one of God's children" (Rom. 8:16). I endured the stresses of growing up and lived through failure and disappointment. The blessed Comforter, however, has always been there, guiding, directing, and reminding me I am a child of God. For eighty-two years, through crises and conflicts beyond anything I could have foreseen, God has been with me.

II. Filled to Overflowing

The indwelling presence of the Holy Spirit that would be operative in the life of every New Testament believer was given Jesus' disciples on Resurrection Sunday. When Jesus "breathed on them," it was for the disciples the "first fruits of the Spirit" (Rom. 8:23). They were "marked in him with a seal, the promised Holy Spirit" (Eph. 1:13). That was, however, only a part of the story."

There were several thousand people in Jerusalem, all of whom needed to hear the message of the resurrection before leaving for home. Jesus, however, commanded His disciples to "wait for the gift my Father promised." He told them that "in a few days you will be baptized with the Holy Spirit" (Acts 1:4-5). As anxious as they were to launch the new movement which was to become the church, one more thing needed to happen: they had to be filled with, and empowered by, the Holy Spirit.

This baptism "with the Holy Spirit" is well illustrated by what happened in Samaria shortly after Pentecost.

Acts 8:12 tells us that "when they believed Philip as he preached the good news of the kingdom of God and the name of Jesus Christ, they were baptized, both men and women." These were genuine converts, introduced to the Gospel message by one well aware of what God had been doing in the Jerusalem church. Philip had been there on the day of Pentecost and knew what had happened in the upper room. But these were Samaritans! Would God do for them what He had done for the church in Jerusalem?

Philip's report got everyone's attention. The Jerusalem church sent Peter and John to verify their conversion was genuine, that Gentiles, and the hated Samaritans of all people, had "accepted the Word of God" (Acts 8:14). Unbelievable!

Some have argued that the Samaritans were not Christians until after "Peter and John placed their hands on them, and they received the Holy Spirit" (Acts 8:17). We are told, however, that "they all paid close attention" to what was said (vs. 6), that "there was great joy in that city" (vs. 8), they "believed Philip as he preached" (vs. 12), "were baptized both men and women" (vs. 12), and that they "had accepted the word of God" (vs. 14). These are all terms used elsewhere in the New Testament to indicate a genuine conversion experience.

Once that issue was settled, Peter and John then determined that "the Holy Spirit had not yet come upon any of them" (Acts 8:16). They then "placed their hands on them, and they received the Holy Spirit" (Acts 8:17). We are not told they "spoke with tongues" as at Pentecost, but it is clear something dramatic happened. Simon the Sorcerer was so impressed that he offered them money "so that everyone on whom I lay my hands may receive the Holy Spirit" (Acts 8:19).

It is to be regretted that the issue of "tongues," known by some as their "prayer language," has clouded one of the most profound and moving personal experiences available to the growing believer.

There is no discussion, in either the book of Acts or in 1 Corinthians, as to whether one *must* speak in tongues, either in worship or as evidence of having been filled with the Spirit. It was not the issue it has now become; it was simply a part of the package.

> Since speaking in tongues was a repeated expression of this dynamic, or charismatic, dimension of the coming of the Spirit, the contemporary Christian may expect this, too, as a part of his or her experience in the Spirit. If the Pentecostal may not say one must speak in tongues, the Pentecostal may surely say, why not speak in tongues? It does have repeated biblical precedent, it did have evidential value at Cornelius' household (Acts 10:45-46), and—in spite of much that has been written to the contrary—it does have value both for the edification of the believer (1 Cor. 14:2-4) and, with interpretation, for the edification of the church (1 Cor. 14:5, 26-28) (Fee, *Gospel and Spirit*, 99).

In her book, *Something More,* Catherine Marshall recounts that, following a study on the work of the Holy Spirit in the ministry of Jesus and the early church, she opened her life to

The Making of a Model

the work of the Spirit in a way she had never experienced before.

> Because the Holy Spirit is a living, always-contemporary Personality, down all the centuries there must be an ever-unfolding manifestation of Jesus, His personality, His ways of dealing with us along with new, fresh disclosures of the mind of the Father. I found this concept endlessly provocative ... and I still do. ... So very simply, I asked for the gift of the Helper, thanked Him for granting this, and entered upon ... living out of this new relationship. I experienced no waves of emotion or ecstasy. Even when eighteen years later, I was given the gift of a heavenly language (glossolalia), it was with no particular fanfare; rather as a divine quartermaster might casually hand out a tool for a job, 'Here. You'll need this' (270-271).

I am aware that many of the outstanding men and women who have been blessed with remarkable ministries — Jonathan Edwards, John Wesley, Mother Theresa, and Billy Graham — are among those in the annals of church history who have never claimed, to my knowledge, to have experienced this aspect of the Holy Spirit's work. They were committed to the authority of God's Word and open to everything God had for them. And yet, influenced perhaps by their training and understanding of the Scriptures, they never realized the Pentecostal experience is still valid for us today.

Although vitally important to the ministry of the Holy Spirit in and through the body of Christ, I have chosen to say very little about the gifts of the Spirit. Paul, in one of his "lists," enumerates nine gifts: a word of wisdom, a word of knowledge, faith, gifts of healing, working of miracles, prophecy, the discerning of spirits, tongues, and the interpretation of tongues (1 Cor. 12:8-10). These are critical to the manifestation of God within the body of believers, but I will leave that discussion to another forum.

My attitude toward the fruit of the Spirit, however, has been a different matter entirely.

The gifts are "manifestations of the Spirit given for the common good" (1 Cor. 12:7). These gifts reflect God's empowerment in, for, and through the body of believers. The fruit, on the other hand, are personal, reflecting our maturity and character. And whereas the gifts of the Spirit are given at the moment, and as they are needed, the fruit of the Spirit are developed gradually through times of testing, trial, and service.

The fruit are, in fact, nothing less than the disposition and character of the Master Himself. In Gal. 5:22-23, the Apostle Paul specifies the fruit of the Spirit as being love, joy, peace, patience, kindness, goodness, faithfulness, gentleness, and self-control. All these, and more, were exemplified in the life of our Lord.

In Romans 8:9-11, the Apostle Paul refers to the Holy Spirit as the Spirit of Christ.

> You, however, are controlled not by the sinful nature but by the Spirit, if the Spirit of God lives in you. And if anyone does not have the Spirit of Christ, he does not belong to Christ.

In my pursuit of the active ministry of the Spirit in my life, my quest has centered on the fruit of the Spirit. Love, joy, and peace seem to go with my Christian experience. But patience and gentleness and self-control? You have to be kidding! I want to model the Master but discover that when it comes to these critical dispositions of the Spirit, I need divine help.

In my drive to model the Master, I am seldom confused as to what is expected of me. The pattern I am called to follow I find in Jesus' character and disposition. The problem, however, is that I can never get away from the conflict between my self-interest and the Jesus-centered attitude the Spirit wants to develop in my life.

And, I discover, I am not alone. Like almost every other Christian I know, I find that even after surrendering my life to Christ, self-centeredness keeps coming back to the surface for a new breath of fresh air. My carnal nature keeps haunting me with drives and interests that have no place in my life. So then, what am I to do? Paul's answer is direct and to the point. "So I say, live by the Spirit and you will not gratify the desires of the sinful nature" (Gal. 5:15). The battle, I discover, between my selfish ambitions and the character of Jesus is never-ending and can only be settled by the Spirit of Christ.

If we are to successfully model the Master, this is where our modeling begins.

There is much more that I could say if I were attempting to give a comprehensive picture of the Spirit's ministry in and through the people of God. Before we conclude this discussion, however, I do want to comment on the place of the Spirit in public worship.

13 – The Go-Between Spirit

The church, in the Apostle Paul's view, was a worshipping community. And the essence of their worship was the active presence of the Holy Spirit.

Much of the discussion and resistance to the work of the Spirit in the modern American church stems from the abuse that has been made of this precious gift of God. I am convinced that if we duplicated the Biblical pattern in the modern Church, the blessing it would bring to our congregations would alter this conversation.

In her book, *Lead Me, Holy Spirit,* Stormie Omartian tells of the Spirit-filled worship she encountered attending the Church on the Way in Van Nuys, CA.

> I sensed something remarkable the moment I walked into the sanctuary. I could not identify it at first. But I soon learned it was the presence of the Holy Spirit of God. And it was palpable. ... It was dynamic and life-changing. It was the power of God's love, joy, and peace enveloping us. ... It was the presence of God washing over you — cleansing, refreshing, strengthening, clarifying. ... Nothing weird ever happened at church. ... The Holy Spirit was unmistakably the center of it all, and people soaked up His presence like sponges. It didn't make us strange; it made us more normal. It didn't make us act crazy; it made us more sober-minded. It didn't make us attract people's attention; it made us forget ourselves and focus entirely on the Lord in praise and worship" (10).

I know what Stormie is writing about.

It was during my first year at Central Bible College in Springfield, Missouri, that a spiritual revival swept the campus. It began, as I recall, with public confession of sin as

God began to speak to us in an extraordinary way. The most moving memory of those days was a chapel service in which the presence of God was unmistakable. Hundreds of young people stood in dead silence and in absolute awe, conscious of a Divine Presence that left us speechless. Forgotten were the refreshments in the cafeteria, morning classes, or job assignments. We stood, stark still, silent in the presence of Almighty God.

Suddenly, interrupting the quiet, a young lady began to give what we understood to be a "message in tongues." No gibberish, no loud voice, but a free-flowing statement in a language that neither she nor any of us understood. As soon as she quieted, a gentleman, standing in another part of the auditorium, began to "interpret" into English what she had said. It was one of the few times in my Christian experience that I felt I had heard from God, speaking in terms I could understand, and in a manner that resonated with my spirit. A Buddhist could have been in the congregation that day and, although he would not have understood what was happening, he would have been profoundly moved. This was real.

III. Only a Beginning

My experience with the Holy Spirit began when I was fourteen years of age. I was a typical teenager, immature and with glaring personality weaknesses, some of which, to my chagrin, are with me still. But I was hungry for everything God had for me. I still recall going to the altar following a

13 – The Go-Between Spirit

Sunday evening service and seeking God late into the night for His anointing.

And, yes, I began to worship God that evening — and only occasionally since — in a language I did not understand. Far from being gibberish or an ecstatic, emotional outburst, it was a moving time of surrender and commitment to the call of God. To this youngster, it was a meaningful and life-changing encounter with the Living God.

But it was only a beginning, an initial experience in my walk with God. God knew what lay ahead, and already, though I was only a fourteen-year-old boy, He was preparing me for a future I could never have imagined. The day would come when I would need His comforting presence if I were to maintain my faith and preserve my sanity.

As I reflect on those tumultuous years, I cannot reconstruct the process whereby I was able to get my life back on track. Modeling the Master had taken a most unexpected turn. But slowly, imperceptibly, quietly, new hope emerged. The sleeper on my truck became a sanctuary and I credit the Holy Spirit for gently prodding me, encouraging me to forget the past, forgive myself, and come back into full fellowship with God.

Bob Fu, in his book, *God's Double Agent*, tells of an experience he once had while serving as a leader in the House Church movement in China. To help implement much-needed training for his coworkers, Bob helped establish a Christian Training Center in Beijing.

In one session, American evangelist Ronny Lewis was leading them in a study of Hebrews 6. He had just quoted verse 19, "We have this hope as an anchor for the soul, firm and secure," when, according to Bob Fu,

> Just as the words were coming out of his mouth, I felt a breeze on my face, looked up, and was surprised that no windows had been opened. My coworkers looked up from their notes as well. Suddenly a very strong wind, like you might feel while standing by an ocean, filled that Beijing apartment. ... As the wind whipped around us, we began praying aloud and crying out to God. People began speaking in what sounded like other languages, which was very much at odds with my solid Presbyterian training. As I called out to God, however, the Holy Spirit came upon me and I too spoke in tongues. A peace and comfort surrounded me, and I was filled with unspeakable joy (183).

This experience is real.

As it is written, 'No eye has seen, no ear has heard, no mind has conceived what God has prepared for those who love him — but God has revealed it to us by his Spirit (1 Cor. 2:10).

God, I am convinced, is eager to reveal Himself ... and He will do so whenever He finds an open heart.

– Strategies for Living #9 –
The Mistake of My Life

It was on a Sunday morning in early spring 1978 that I made the mistake of my life. Ignorant of the consequences, it took but ten minutes to announce a decision that changed the course of my life.

I had been the pastor of Trinity Temple since its beginning in 1968. As the founding pastor, I had suffered through the early days when I never knew for sure whether this venture of faith would survive. Staff turnover, friends who came and went, financial stress, and the challenge of speaking three times a week had all left their toll. I was tired beyond belief and ready to run.

On a chilly Sunday morning in March 1978, I submitted my letter of resignation. After ten years of ministry to Central Pennsylvania, I was leaving. It is now difficult to understand the thinking that went into that decision, but it seemed right at the time. And I am haunted by "what if?"

I devastated my family. My wife was becoming more involved in our church's ministry and our daughter was approaching her last year of high school. Despite fierce opposition, I decided to return to Seminary and complete my education. There was nothing in the move, however, that made any sense to either my family or my congregation. And they were right.

The Making of a Model

I share my story for I am not alone in making a decision that turned out to have had catastrophic consequences. None of us is free from doing things we will always regret. The question isn't whether we have erred; the question is, "What have we done about it?" The temptation, of course, is to blame others and play the martyr. It is only when we are honest enough to accept responsibility for our actions, however, that we will be able to reconstruct.

W. E. Maxwell, in his book, *Failing Forward*, writes that "no matter how difficult your problems were, the key to overcoming them doesn't lie in changing your circumstances. It's in changing yourself. That in itself is a process, and it begins with a desire to be teachable. If you're willing to do that, then you'll be able to handle failure. From this moment on, make a commitment to do whatever it takes to fail forward" (7).

Leaving Trinity Temple was truly the mistake of my life, the one decision over which I have often agonized. But when I look at where and who I am today, I am encouraged. I am a different man, and my relationship with my family and with God is now stronger and more fulfilling than it has ever been. And I'm writing about it—to people just like me!

– 14 –

The Final State

Life as it was Meant to Be

We are children of God, and what we will be has not yet been made known. But we know that when he appears, we shall be like him, for we shall see him as he is.

1 John 3:2

THE CITY OF CUSCO had shut down for the day, and in the quiet of a normal Andean night, things were deathly still. It was 1949, and at 11,000 feet in elevation, the nights were bitterly cold, and the streets were empty.

An Andean enclave of some 60,000 residents, Cusco was still years away from achieving its world-renowned status. All around the city, reminders of Cusco's Inca heritage and subsequent occupation by the Spanish could still be found. And high on a mountain, the ruins of Saqsayhuaman, the ancient Inca citadel overlooking the city, could be seen, standing like a sentinel, over this former capital of the Inca Empire. And nearby, a towering statue of Christ overlooked the city with open arms. I should have been impressed but, to this ten-year-old, it was just home.

There was one night during the two years we lived there I shall never forget.

I remember awakening with a start, disturbed by a loud, rumbling sound outside our home. It was, more than likely, a group of drunken natives enjoying an evening of revelry on the way to their next stop. As the group came closer, the noise intensified. I could hear them cheering and laughing as they passed by. And then, as they slowly faded into the distance … silence.

I am not sure what prompted the thought, but suddenly I sat up in bed in a cold sweat. One horrifying thought overwhelmed this ten-year-old boy: "Jesus has come for His own! The church has been raptured, and I've been left behind!"

But I wasn't … and I continue to await the day when "we who are still alive and are left will be caught up with them in the clouds to meet the Lord in the air (1 Thess. 4:17). I am well aware the day of my departure may come at any time, and I'm excited about the prospect. One way or another my death――and new life―is but a few years away. Soon, I plan to hear my Savior say, "Welcome home, Larry. The battle's over!"

I cannot put into words my gratitude for what God has done in my life. Only by the goodness of God am I among those living with the "blessed hope" of finally achieving the Christlikeness for which I have spent a lifetime praying. With the rapture or my death, my *earthly* pilgrimage will be over. My drive toward becoming a living model of the Master will have come to a successful, triumphant end. I will, in the fullest sense of the word, be the *perfect man* I was created to be.

My journey is neither completed nor complete, however, and I will not be satisfied until I am able to join with all God's people as we rally around the heavenly throne in the celebration for which all of creation has been waiting: the crowning of Jesus Christ as Lord of Lord's and King of Kings.

> The seventh angel sounded his trumpet, and there were loud voices in heaven, which said: The kingdom of the world has become the kingdom of our Lord and of his Christ, and he will reign for ever and ever (Rev. 11:15).

Jesus Christ, as promised at the time of His ascension, will return to earth. But He comes, no longer as a sacrificial lamb; He returns as conquering King.

Oh! What a day that will be!

I. The Second Coming of Christ

The return of our Lord, however, will not take place until the Church has been removed from the world and society has been given the opportunity to rule without the mellowing influence of God and His people.

Following the rapture of the Church, and in an attempt to bring a measure of tranquility to society, the man of sin will

The Making of a Model

negotiate a final settlement to the Arab-Israeli conflict and bring about a time of remarkable peace on earth.

The Antichrist, this "man of sin" (2 Thess. 2:3), will be a cultured, respectable, brilliant statesman. If I understand Daniel 9:27 correctly, he will make a seven-year treaty with the people of Israel. The Jews will be allowed to rebuild the Temple in Jerusalem, and for three and one-half years, there will be peace in the Middle East. At that point, however, something will trigger a change in attitude toward the Jewish people. The Antichrist will renounce the treaty at the three-and-one-half-year mark, and all hell will break loose!

But as the Antichrist turns on the Jewish people, he fails to reckon with the fact they are still the people of God. In attacking them, he has challenged the forces of heaven. He may not believe in God, and he may feel himself invincible, but things will begin to happen over which he has no control.

> For then there will be great distress, unequaled from the beginning of the world until now – and never to be equaled again. If those days had not been cut short, no one would survive, but for the sake of the elect those days will be shortened (Matt. 24:21-22).

Two angels, on the day of Jesus' ascension, had this great day in view when they told the disciples,

> Men of Galilee, why do you stand here looking into the sky? This same Jesus, who has been taken from you into heaven, will come back in the same way you have seen him go into heaven (Acts. 1:10-11).

14 – The Final State

The second coming of Jesus Christ, however, is more than a confirmation, or completion, of the first. It marks a *new* work of God. The Kingdom of God, introduced and initiated during His first sojourn on earth, will finally be fully established. This time Jesus comes, not as the humble carpenter from Nazareth, but as the royal Son of God. The King is back! Attempts have been made to spiritualize Jesus' return, but there is solid evidence John was writing of a literal event.

> He is coming with the clouds, and every eye will see Him, including those who pierced Him, and all the families of earth will mourn over Him (Rev. 1:7).

That statement would have been difficult to understand a few years ago. But the development of the internet, satellite technology, and the common use of cell phones have made it easy to visualize how "all the families of the earth" will see the appearance of our Lord when He "comes with clouds." As He stands on the Mount of Olives, "every eye" will *see* Him. All creation will finally acknowledge the Lion from the tribe of Judah, the promised Messiah, Son of Man and Son of God, resplendent in all His glory!

He will be coming, however, at a time when the world is in turmoil. The State of Israel, under attack by forces that will come against her "out of the north" (Dan. 11:40), and facing extermination, will finally acknowledge Jesus as their Messiah. Their survival will be assured when the forces of heaven fight on their behalf in what is known as the Battle of Armageddon (Rev. 16:12-16).

This is the battle that was foreseen by the Prophet Ezekiel.

> This is what will happen in that day: When Gog attacks the land of Israel, my hot anger will be aroused, declares the Sovereign LORD. In my zeal and fiery wrath I declare that at that time there shall be a great earthquake in the land of Israel. ... The mountains will be overturned, the cliffs will crumble and every wall will fall to the ground. I will summon a sword against Gog on all my mountains, declares the Sovereign LORD. Every man's sword will be against his brother. I will execute judgment on him with plague and bloodshed; I will pour down torrents of rain, hailstones and burning sulfur on him and on his troops and on the many nations with him (Ezek. 38:18-22).

Satan and the forces of evil will be defeated, and life on earth will be established as it was meant to be from the very beginning. The fall of man may have delayed the implementation of what God had in mind for the human family, but God will not be denied. Finally, this world will be God's world!

In Revelation 20:2-3, we read,

> He seized the dragon, that ancient serpent, who is the devil, or Satan, and bound him for a thousand years. He threw him into the Abyss, and locked and sealed it over him, to keep him from deceiving the nations anymore until the thousand years were ended.

II. The Millennial Kingdom

I believe in a literal, one-thousand-year period during which divine rule will be established on earth. Satan will be bound, and worldwide peace and harmony, absent since those early days in the Garden of Eden, will finally prevail.

14 – The Final State

In Genesis 1:31, we are told that "God saw all that he had made and it was very good."

God never meant for the history of mankind to evolve as it has. The Garden of Eden was only the beginning of a plan that could only have been conceived by the mind of God. Human family life, work responsibilities, business, and commerce, were all meant to develop in the centuries to follow under divine direction. The Garden sojourn was only a beginning, an introduction, the first step toward a life-long, active partnership between God and His creation.

But then came the imposition of a condition. "You are free to eat from any tree in the garden," God told Adam and Eve, "but you must not eat from the tree of the knowledge of good and evil" (Gen. 2:16-17). The "fruit" was not the issue; the issue was their voluntary surrender to the will of God. And Adam and Eve made a fateful choice. Rather than obey the mandate, they decided the fruit was just too good to refuse. It was a simple act, and it took but five minutes of their time, but the results were catastrophic. In this one act of disobedience, their lives and the history of mankind were changed forever.

That such an act could so devastate the human family tells us much of how God views the sin of self-will. God has given us firm directives designed to protect us from ourselves. We are free to ignore Him if we wish, but we do so only to our peril. Sin is a vicious taskmaster, and God knows, left to ourselves we are prone to self-destruct. It is not that He wishes to limit our freedom; He wants to preserve it.

The Making of a Model

God designed man with a free will, and rightly so. Obedience, however, must come from the heart; love, by definition, must always be a matter of choice.

Adam and Eve were given the ability and intelligence to make plans and to accomplish objectives worthy of one created by the mind of God. But they rebelled, and almost everything God intended to do for them and their descendants was put on hold.

The influence of evil was so complete Genesis 6:5 tells us that "the Lord saw how great the wickedness of the human race had become on the earth, and that every inclination of the human heart was only evil all the time." When we compare the days of divine presence in the Garden to the days of wickedness that followed, we can see what happens when man chooses to live without God.

The human family was beyond rescue. God then chose to give mankind a fresh start through Noah and his family, and thus the great flood and the death of all but eight people. Whereas God had initially implemented a relationship with two individuals, He now turned to work through the family unit. But that plan fragmented as well, so God turned to the people of Israel and called on them to reveal His greatness and communicate His message.

That nation, however, failed in its mission as well. But God did not abandon His creation. "In the fulness of time, God sent His Son ... to redeem those under law, that we might receive the full rights of sons" (Gal. 4:4). Again, God turned to the people of Israel and again launched an initiative

14 – The Final State

destined to make them the instruments of righteousness to the human race. But they refused His invitation and put His Son to death. And so, finally, God turned to the Church and called on the "people belonging to God [to] declare the praises of him who called you out of darkness into his wonderful light" (1 Pet. 2:9).

The people of Israel may have turned their backs on God's great gift, but they remain the objects of His love. The Prophets make it clear that, as we have already indicated, there is coming a day when the nation will welcome Jesus as their Messiah.

One reason I am convinced there will be a literal, divine rule on earth lasting one thousand years, is what we find in the prophets' message.

> The wolf will live with the lamb, the leopard will lie down with the goat, the calf and the lion and the yearling together; and a little child will lead them" (Isa. 11:8).

> The desert and the parched land will be glad; the wilderness will rejoice and blossom. Like the crocus, it will burst into bloom; it will rejoice greatly and shout for joy. The glory of Lebanon will be given to it, the splendor of Carmel and Sharon; they will see the glory of the Lord, the splendor of our God (Isa. 35:1-2).

Ezekiel wrote of a day when the people of Israel would return to their homeland and become one nation under God.

> For I will take you out of the nations; I will gather you from all the countries and bring you back into your own land. ... I will give you a new heart and put a new spirit in you; I will remove from you your heart of stone and give you a new

heart of flesh. And I will put my Spirit in you and move you to follow my decrees and be careful to keep my laws (Ezek. 36:24, 26-27)

And Israel, in a move that many considered a miracle, *did* return to their homeland in 1948. The spiritual revival of which Ezekiel wrote, however, has not happened and will not until the nation of Israel faces extinction at the end of the seven-year tribulation period. Jesus, then, will come to their rescue and the people of Israel will once again become the people of God.

Following the millennial period, and again, providing I am reading the prophetic record correctly, Satan will be released, and mankind will again turn away from God. And then, in His final act against the forces of hell and sin, God will initiate the great white throne judgment (Rev. 20:11).

With that, God will finally bring about what He had in mind for His own from the very beginning.

III. A New Heaven and a New Earth

Eight individuals emerged from the ark following the great flood and stepped into a pristine environment. But mankind mismanaged the earth's resources and left our world defaced by the demands of modern society.

But God is going to bring His creation back to the state in which He left it on the sixth day of creation.

> Then I saw a new heaven and a new earth, for the first heaven and the first earth had passed away, and there was no longer any sea. I saw the Holy City, the new Jerusalem,

coming down out of heaven dressed for her husband. And I heard a loud voice from the throne saying, "Look! God's dwelling place is now among the people, and he will dwell with them. They will be his people, and God himself will be with them and be their God" (Rev. 21:1-3).

Man has corrupted the marvelous creation given him by the creative hand of God. Pollution, human filth, and environmental mismanagement have left their mark. But all will be purified by fire. Remnants of our current world will be destroyed. It will, indeed, be a "new heavens and a new earth."

That perspective is given us by the Apostle Peter.

But the day of the Lord will come like a thief. The heavens will disappear with a roar; the elements will be destroyed by fire, and the earth and everything in it will be laid bare. Since everything will be destroyed in this way, what kind of people ought you to be? You ought to live holy and godly lives as you look forward to the day of God and speed its coming. That day will bring about the destruction of the heavens by fire, and the elements will melt in the heat. But in keeping with his promise we are looking forward to a new heaven and a new earth, the home of righteousness (2 Peter 3:10-13).

The old order will give way to a new creation, free from the remnants of human history. The human family will have come full circle and will fellowship with the Sovereign God just as did Adam and Eve in the Garden. The glory of heaven and the majesty of God will have come to earth.

When John writes, "I saw the "Holy City, the new Jerusalem, coming down out of heaven from God, prepared as a bride beautifully dressed for her husband" (Rev. 21:2), he describes a move of God that fits into no frame of reference with which we are familiar. The grandeur of what God has in mind for His own is greater than anything we could imagine.

Despite the ravages of war that will emerge out of the tribulation period, God will not abandon His creation; He is going to restore it. Just as He planned from the beginning, He is going to "bring all things in heaven and earth together under one head, even Christ" (Eph. 1:10).

God knew the end from the beginning. He was well aware that Adam and Eve would rebel and that Israel would disavow her special relationship with God by crucifying His Son. *But*, and this "but" makes all the difference in the world ...

> But Christ has indeed been raised from the dead, the firstfruits of those who have fallen asleep. ... For as in Adam all die, so in Christ all will be made alive. ... Then the end will come, when he hands over the kingdom to God the Father after he has destroyed all dominion, authority and power. For he must reign until he has put all his enemies under his feet. The last enemy to be destroyed is death. ... When he has done this, then the Son himself will be made subject to him who put everything under him, so that God may be all in all (1 Cor. 15:20, 22, 24-25, 28)

God's plan to establish an intimate relationship with man, a state in which the glory of the Godhead might be shared with His creation, will one day come to pass. The Apostle Paul wrote of how "God has chosen to make known among the Gentiles [that's us] the glorious riches of this mystery, which is *Christ in you, the hope of glory*" (Col. 1:27).

That is a marvelous hope, an encouragement to each of us no matter what our station in life. There is light at the end of our tunnel; a new day is coming! One of these days, perhaps soon, all of life's pressures will be behind us.

Until then, however, God has privileged us to serve as living models of the Master. It is a mission that is, indeed, beyond every one of us. We are all abominably human, fighting our own battles, struggling to emulate the pattern set by our Lord. We can scarcely measure up to our own standards, much less those we have seen exemplified in the Person of Jesus Christ. We must, however, never but never give up! God will not give up on us, and we must never give up on Him!

My track record has been a difficult one, but I believe in a God of second chances, a God Who is still in the business of doing the impossible. With the Apostle Paul, I confess that,

> I want to know Christ and the power of his resurrection and the fellowship of sharing in his sufferings, becoming like him in his death ... forgetting what is behind and straining toward what is ahead, I press on toward the goal to win the prize for which God has called me heavenward in Christ Jesus (Phil. 3:10-11, 13-14).

And *that* is what *The Making of a Model* is all about.

God has been good to me, and from the smoldering ruin of my life, I have recycled and found the strength to live again. I am slowly, but most definitely, becoming a living model of the Master.

The Making of a Model

It has been an eighty-two-year journey with a track record marked by the good, the bad, and occasionally, just a touch of the ugly. But I do not complain, and I'm not alone. Although I have been writing in the first person, everything that applies to me applies to you too. I trust you are with me as together we build on what has been toward a future in which our dreams come true.

I believe God had a purpose for my life when He created me. Implementing that purpose may have been delayed, but it has not changed. Not only do I serve a God of the impossible, I serve a God Who has little respect for time. What got off track forty years ago is back on track again.

I've been through the hurricane, and the storms have threatened to sink my ship. But I have chosen to put a positive twist on my past and see God's hand in my journey; it has helped me become a better man. God, it seems, knew He had to grow me before He could grow my future.

Jesus Christ has given my sunset years the glow of an early morning sun, and I want that to be your story as well. When the going gets rough, when honesty causes you to cringe in shame, when missed opportunities and failed endeavors haunt you, I want the story of my life to help you know there is hope for a tomorrow brighter than your brightest dreams.

What God has done for me, He can do for you, too. Our God is available, and more than willing, to take you, as you are, and to make of you ... as He is of me ...

A living model of Jesus Christ.

– Strategies for Living #10 –
Thirty Years Down ... and Thirty to Go

Thirty years ago, April 29, 1991, I was into my first year as a commercial truck driver with Werner Enterprises out of Omaha, NE, the beginning of a lifestyle that would last fourteen years. My career and my personal life were all on the line on that day in 1991; I could only hope it was the start of something good.

It was Monday in America, and George H. W. Bush was president. Gas was $1.14 per gallon, a 1st class stamp was $.29, and the Dow Jones Average hit 3168.83. Popular TV shows included Cheers, Roseanne, and Simpson and Son.

None of which was of much concern to me. I would soon move to the Seattle area to live on Angelica, my 40-ft sailboat. I would see the country from corner to corner, be honored with a one-million-mile-accident-free award, survive prostate cancer, remarry my sweetheart, purchase a home in New Hampshire, and finally, retire debt-free to dedicate my final years to writing the story of my life.

Thirty years! In the span of a lifetime, an interlude that came and went far more quickly than you would think. But for me the issue is not where I have been; the issue now is where I am going. I can agonize over past failures, wallow in self-pity, and surrender to guilt ... or I can face the future with a new attitude. I plan to make these the best, most productive years of my life. Heaven awaits!

And what about you? Can you remember where you were thirty years ago? How well have you lived the last thirty years? Are you a better, wiser, more mature person for having lived the last thirty years, or are they years you'd rather forget?

But the question remains, and this is *the* question: where will be you be thirty years from now? Your last thirty, whether you like it or not, have set you up for the next thirty and will surely influence where you will be in 2051. But they do not determine, they do not make certain, where you will be. That is what your today is all about. The choice is up to you.

One thing is for certain. Like it or not, you will be somewhere on this date thirty years from now. Either you will still be living, or you will have joined the men and women who were here thirty years ago but are no longer with us. George Bush, Doris Day, Carl Sagan, Whitney Houston, Stephen Hawking, Mother Teresa, Billy Graham, Kobe Bryant, and Bob Hope are just a few that come to mind. They are now set for eternity in an existence that has been determined, not by how well they lived, but by what they did with Jesus Christ.

Jesus said, "Let not your heart be troubled. In my Father's house are many mansions, and I go to prepare a place for you, that where I am you may be also." He awaits your decision, for He has prepared for you an existence your mind cannot imagine. This is reality; it will happen. And what it will mean will be determined by what you do now with Jesus Christ.

Epilogue

JONI EARECKSON TADA was rapidly reaching a crisis point. Quadriplegic from the age of seventeen as the result of a diving accident, she had fought years of chronic pain, breast cancer, had had a mastectomy, and had now contracted pneumonia.

"The second night, Ken and Joni came to a time that seemed to be the 'worst of the worst' of what they had faced together through the years. It was an anguished, turbulent nightmare of a night, as Joni's pain, weakness, claustrophobia, and nasal and lung congestion launched simultaneous attacks on her body. ...

"It was a grim, dark path for both of them. Life for them had never been what you would call easy, but this seemed more like David's "valley of the shadow of death" than anything they had ever experienced. ...

"On the third near-sleepless night for them both, Joni woke her husband for the fifth time — once again, she needed help blowing her nose. Lying in bed, gravity was her enemy and her lungs were filling up faster than she could expel the phlegm. ...

"'Ken, I'm seeing spots,' she mumbled, 'I can't ... breathe' her voice trailed off. ... Joni wheezed and then dropped her head again. ... 'Don't give up now,' Ken almost shouted. 'Don't quit on me—you can do it. BREATHE!' He gave another hard push on her abdomen. *'Come on, Joni! Breathe!'* ... There was a rasping sound in her chest, but a few minutes later, she was able to expel more phlegm. ... Both began to breathe easier.

"Just before Joni drifted off to sleep, she sensed that the approaching hours would be particularly intense. ... In the dark, in a whisper so as to not awaken Ken, she prayed, *'Lord, I'm afraid it'll be worse next time. Would You show up in some special way? When I wake up an hour or two from now – and I know I will – please let me see You, feel You. I need You, Jesus! Let me know that You're there and that You're with me.'*

Later that same night, when she awakened again, pain seemed to fill the whole room. ... She called Ken, and he came to her, stepping into the dim illumination of the bedside lamp. ... Suddenly, Joni turned her head and looked up at him, eyes wide with wonder.

"It took him by surprise. Was she hallucinating? What was she seeing.?

'You're Him!' she said.

"I ... I don't understand, Joni."

'Ken ... you're Him! You're Jesus!'

Fresh tears began to flow, and he dabbed them from her face with a tissue. 'I'm not kidding. I can feel His touch when you touch me. I can see Him in your smile. I can hear Him in the tone of your voice. Right now! I mean it,' she said with a sob. 'This is what I prayed for. You are Jesus!'" (Eareckson Tada, *Joni and Ken*, 190-191).

In the worst of times, in the darkest night, indeed, Jesus *was* there, seen in the gentle touch, the call for courage, and the encouraging word ... given by a godly man called Ken.

We used to sing, "What the world needs is Jesus; just a glimpse of Him." Never was that more true than the day in which we live. And, indeed, He can be found ... in the lives of men and women like you and me ... called, anointed, empowered, and sanctified,

Living models of Jesus Christ!

"Now to the King eternal, immortal, invisible, the only God, be honor and glory for ever and ever. Amen" (1 Tim. 1:17).

Appendix

On Becoming a Living Model of the Master

IT WAS A BEAUTIFUL morning in Central Pennsylvania, one of those days when it just feels good to be alive. A close friend I shall call Susan had agreed to meet me at the Perkin's Restaurant in Wormleysburg, and with a quick "hello" to the manager, a close friend to both of us, we made our way to a back table. Little did we know that over the next forty-five minutes, amid the sounds of animated conversations and the noise typical to a hungry mid-morning crowd, the eternal future of one lady—and, a few weeks later, her husband—was about to change forever.

Throughout this work, I have been highlighting the privilege that is ours to become living models of Jesus Christ. It may seem an impossible dream, but no matter where we are in our spiritual journey, God wants to do something spectacular in your life and mine. "As it is written: 'No eye has seen, no ear has heard, no mind has conceived what God has prepared for those who love him'" (1 Cor. 2:9). And the transition, from who we are to what we can be, begins the day we surrender our lives, entirely and without reservation, to the Lordship of Jesus Christ.

The Making of a Model

That experience, the foundation for everything I have highlighted in The Making of a Model, is defined in the Gospel of John as being "born again" (John 3:3). In the words of the Apostle Paul, "if anyone is in Christ, he is a new creation; the old has gone, the new has come! (2 Cor. 5:17).

Much of what I have written about the Christian faith makes little sense to those who have no awareness of personal sin, feel no need for forgiveness, and have little interest in a relationship with God. Such, however, was not the case with Susan.

For many years in rebellion against her Christian upbringing, she had seen that life away from God is no walk in the park. Life had been difficult, and now, finally, Susan was open to the Gospel and anxious to establish a new relationship with Jesus Christ.

She did not invite Christ to be her Lord that day, and I did not press the issue. But God was at work, and it wasn't long before she and her husband, through a simple prayer of surrender, invited Jesus Christ to be the Lord of their lives.

I began my conversation with Susan by reminding her that God has an amazing plan for each of our lives. It is uniquely tailored to our personality, our gender, our abilities, our age, our training, and our station in life.

And it all begins with the most earth-shaking, life-changing experience any of us have ever had: the gift, here and now, of new life in Jesus Christ.

The kicker, however, is that this experience is not something we can earn or deserve. The Bible says that we are "saved through faith ... It is the gift of God, not by works so that no one may boast" (Eph. 2:8,9).

To us, it would seem that we should be able, indeed, that we must be required to do something to earn it. But when we see what the Bible says about sin, we see that this is not only the way it is but the only way it can be.

Most of us would agree that we have each done things we know to be wrong. We have sinned.

I often wonder how often the normal man sins, that is, thinks, or does something he instinctively knows to be wrong. Ten times a day? Five times a day? If we did what we instinctively knew to be wrong only three times a day, that's over 1,000 times a year.

Each time we sin, our character is twisted ever so slightly, so much so that sin becomes to us like a spiritual cancer that pervades every part of our being. A person with this dreaded disease cannot find healing by thinking good thoughts; it takes outside intervention, often through an operation, chemotherapy, or radiation. Likewise, we cannot deal with the sin problem by going to church or turning over a new leaf. We need outside help!

Fortunately for us, God loves us. Indeed, He loves us so much that He wants to forgive our sin. But that brings up a problem. God is just, and He would like to forgive us, but sin cannot be so easily dismissed. Sin has created a problem for Him and for us. He is a loving God who wants to forgive our sin, but is, at the same time, a just God who cannot dismiss our sin as if it never happened. Sin carries a penalty that cannot be overlooked. In the Old Testament, we are told "the soul who sins is the one who will die" (Ezek. 18:4), and in the New, "the wages of sin is death" (Rom. 6:23). In both places, death is indicated.

Now to understand this "death," we must go back to the Garden of Eden where God told Adam and Eve that if they ate from a particular forbidden tree, they would surely die. They did eat but they did not drop dead. What happened to them was that they were expelled from the Garden; they became separated from God. And that is what has happened to you and me.

Let me explain.

Each of us is a three-part being; we have a body, a soul, and a spirit; that is, we are physical, intellectual, and spiritual beings. When Adam and Eve "died," they didn't drop dead, and they did not suddenly lose their minds. What did happen was that their spirits ceased to be functional; they lost the close relationship they had with God.

In short, the whole point of Christianity — what God wants to do in your life and mine — is to revive this third dimension of our lives, that is, breathing new life to our spirit. Due to the influence of sin, we might say our spirit has been deactivated. We have for too long been chugging along like a six-cylinder auto working on four cylinders, controlled by our physical and intellectual needs. New life in Christ begins, however, when He reactivates our spirit as a controlling force in our lives.

And this is where Jesus Christ comes into the picture.

I believe everything the New Testament says about Jesus: that He was born of a woman who was a literal virgin until after His birth, that He really walked on water and raised the dead, that He really died, and that He rose from the dead three days later. I know that's rather unbelievable, but the Bible is very clear: that is the way it was.

The whole point here is that Jesus came to earth to suffer God's judgment on our sin and on our behalf. It's unbelievable that God should accept Him as our substitute. In that way, however, God is able to judge our sin on the one hand and still forgive us on the other.

One statement Jesus made while He was on the cross says it all. He said, "My God, my God, why have You forsaken me?" (Matt. 27:46). It was the only time in all of eternity that He called His Heavenly Father "God." And, it was the only time He found Himself separated from His Father because of our sin. He was at that time as separated from God as the most ungodly person one can imagine. God abandoned of God is beyond belief!

Fortunately, within a few hours, it was over. He called on God, the relationship reestablished, and said, "Father, into your hands I commit my spirit" (Luke 23:46). The separation on our behalf was over! And He died.

And now it is up to each one of us to accept, by faith, what He has done on our behalf.

I often hear, even from those who are not active Christians, that, "You think I'm a heathen? I believe in God." But that's not the kind of faith the Bible addresses. Faith, the kind of faith that will change a man's life, is not just believing the truth about God. The devil, in fact, believes the truth about God. The Bible says, "You believe there is one God? You do well. The devils also believe, and tremble" (Jas. 2:19).

Faith, the kind of faith that will revolutionize a person's life, is putting our faith in Him and Him alone to forgive us of our sins and to bring us into a right relationship with God.

There is no way we can earn or merit God's forgiveness. And there is no need; Jesus Christ has done it all. All we have to do is accept and receive from Him the forgiveness and the new life He offers.

I know it sounds too simple to be true. But conversion is the greatest miracle I have ever seen. How an ungodly man can be dramatically changed through the means of a simple prayer and act of surrender to the Lordship of Christ is beyond me. I don't understand it; I just know that it works!

Titus 3:5 says, "Not by works of righteousness that we have done, but according to His mercy He has saved us, by the washing of regeneration and the renewing of the Holy Spirit."

Conversion is a two-step process.

First of all, we invite God, through the medium of prayer, to forgive us of our sins and to cleanse us of all that is ungodly in our lives. The New Testament says that "if we confess our sins He is faithful and just to forgive us our sins and to cleanse us from all unrighteousness" (1 John 1:9).

But that is only half the process. We must furthermore ask Him to become the Lord of our lives and pledge to do His will from this point forward to the very best of our ability.

These two steps go hand in hand. We need to be forgiven so that Jesus Christ might become the Lord of our life, but we also need Him to become the Lord of our life so that we might stay forgiven.

Many years ago, after sharing much of what I have written above with a psychology major, she said, "There has to be more to it than that. I haven't figured it out yet, but there must be more."

But there isn't. The conversion experience establishes a relationship with a God who has given His Son to make it possible. It is not all that complicated. The problem is that it involves the total commitment of our will to our benevolent Heavenly Father. That is difficult for us, and it is not a decision that can be taken lightly.

It is telling to note that God has no grandchildren; our faith is not a second-hand religion. Conversion is a decision we much each make for ourselves, a conscious act of surrender to the claims of Christ on our lives.

For me, it was a simple prayer at the knees of my grandmother who asked, "Larry, would you like to invite Jesus into your life?" I was only ten years old, with a ten-year-old understanding, but it was sincerely done and has been a significant force in my life since that day seventy-two years ago.

The Making of a Model

I find it almost beyond comprehension that one's eternal future can be dramatically changed through a simple prayer of surrender to the authority of Jesus Christ.

Within a few weeks, at the conclusion of a morning worship service, Susan and her husband came forward as an act of surrender to the claims of Christ and gave me the incredible privilege of praying with them. It took but a few minutes in time, a simple prayer of surrender, and an open invitation for Jesus Christ to become the Lord of their lives, but it had eternal implications. Leland has now gone on, as we say, "to be with the Lord," his eternal destiny determined through a simple word of prayer that signaled an honest surrender to the Lordship of Jesus Christ.

A classic case in point of how this works is found in the story of William Neal Moore as told by Lee Strobel in his book, *The Case for Faith*.

When Strobel met him in Rome, Georgia, he was a well-respected minister dedicated to helping the hurting. But such had not always been the case.

Few people outside of his congregation were aware that in May of 1984, William Moore was just hours from being electrocuted for a murder he had committed some 16 years before. Breaking into the home of 77-year-old Fredger Stapleton in search of cash Stapleton was known to keep in his bedroom, he was caught in the act, killed Stapleton, and fled with $5,600 in cash. After being apprehended, Moore admitted his guilt and was sentenced to death.

But now ... the rest of the story.

Shortly after his imprisonment, two Christian gentlemen, at the behest of Bill Moore's mother, visited him in prison. They told him about a loving God Who was more than willing to forgive him and give him a new direction in life. Unfortunately, he had never heard of a God who loved him unconditionally, even in view of what he had done. So, Billy Moore soon made a life-changing decision: he invited Jesus Christ to be the Lord of his life.

That decision changed everything! From a wasted life of self-centered living, William Moore became a witness to God's love and mercy. He began sharing his story, counseling his fellow inmates, and leading Bible studies and prayer sessions within the Georgia State Penitentiary. So dramatic was the change in his life that it caught the attention of the Georgia Board of Parole and Pardon. Surprisingly, within hours of his execution, Moore's death sentence was commuted to life in prison. And then, in November 1991, in an action unprecedented in the history of the Board, he was released.

As Lee Strobel sat in his home reflecting on the remarkable change of direction Bill Moore's life had taken, Lee asked him "about the source of his amazing metamorphosis. ... [W]hat was responsible for the transformation of Billy Moore?" 'Plain and simple, it was Jesus Christ,' he declared adamantly. 'He changed me in ways I could never have changed on my own. ... He helped me do the right thing. ... He saved my soul" (Strobel, 2000, 259).

The Making of a Model

This sounds, I realize, like just so much religious spin on the life of a man who was caught. The truth, however, is that in some cases, the consequences of a life lived independently of God catch up with us. Living by our drives and selfish interests may seem to be a path to happiness for a while. Sooner or later, however, we must pay the piper. Those who have had a chance to invite God into the mix will tell you without regret that it is the best decision they have ever made; they can't imagine why they waited so long. What an honor, indeed, it is to know the Living God!

And how about you?

Regardless of where you are in your relationship with God, there is more, much more, He has for you. And the point of departure, the place to initiate this life-changing walk of faith, or to discover the fullness of what it means to be a child of God, begins by inviting Jesus Christ to be the unconditional Lord of your life.

And He would like to make of you, as I am slowly becoming, a living model of Jesus Christ. I know ... that will take a miracle you are thinking ... and you are correct. But it is, undeniably, the greatest miracle of divine intervention I have ever seen. To think that people like you and me—fallible, imperfect, weakened by personality defects we can't seem to overcome—could serve as twentieth-century models of the divine Son of God. Unbelievable!

"To this you were called," wrote the Apostle Peter, "because Christ suffered for you, leaving you an example, that you should follow in his steps" (1 Pet. 2:21).

And then you, too, can join me and millions of other growing Christians, believing God to help us that we might each become,

A LIVING MODEL OF JESUS CHRIST!

Bibliography

Alcorn, Randy. *Heaven*. Carol Stream, Il, Tyndale House Publishers, 2004.

Alcorn, Randy. *If God Is Good: Faith in the Midst of Suffering and Evil*. Colorado Springs, CO: Multnomah Books, 2009.

Aldrich, Joseph C. *Life-Style Evangelism: Crossing Traditional Boundaries to Reach the Unbelieving World*. Colorado Springs, Co: Multnomah Books, 1993.

Archer Jr., Gleason L. *Encyclopedia of Bible Difficulties*. Grand Rapids, MI: Zondervan, 1982.

Barton, David. Original Intent. The Courts, the Constitution, & Religion. Aldo, TX: WallBuilders, 2000.

Barnett, Caroline. *willing to walk on water: step out in faith and let God work miracles through your life*. Tyndale, 2013.

Batterson, Mark. *All In: You are one decision away from a totally different life*. Grand Rapids, MI: Zondervan, 2013.

Blackaby, Henry and Norman. *Experiencing Prayer with Jesus*. Colorado Springs, CO: Multnomah Books, 2006.

Bloesch, Donald G. The Last Things: Resurrection, Judgment, Glory. Downers Grove, Il. InterVarsity Press, 2004.

Blomberg, Craig L. *Can We Still Believe the Bible? An Evangelical Engagement with Contemporary Questions*. Grand Rapids, MI: Brazos Press, 2014.

Blomberg, Craig L. *Jesus and the Gospels*. Nashville: Broadman & Holman Publishers, 1997.

Boa, Kenneth & Robert M. Bowman. *20 Compelling Evidences that God Exists: Discover Why Believing in God Makes So Much Sense*. Colorado Springs, Co: David C. Cook, 2005.

Bock, Darrell L. *Jesus According to Scripture: Restoring the Portrait from the Gospels.* Grand Rapids, MI. Baker Academic, 2002.

Boice, James Montgomery. *Foundations of the Christian Faith: A Comprehensive & Readable Theology.* Leicester, England: InterVarsity Press, 1986.

Bounds, E. M. *The Complete works of E. M., Bounds on Prayer: Experience the Wonders of God through Prayer.* Grand Rapids, MI: Baker Books, 1990, 2004.

Bowman Jr., Robert, and J. Ed Komoszewski. *Putting Jesus in His Place: The Case for the Deity of Christ.* Grand Rapids, MI. Kregel Publications, 2007.

Brown, Raymond F. *Jesus: God and Man.* New York: MacMillan Publishing Co., Inc., 1967.

Bruce, F. F. *Paul: Apostle of the Heart Set Free.* Grand Rapids, MI.: Wm. B. Eerdmans Publishing Company, 1999.

Campolo, Tony. *Wake Up America!* Answering God's radical call while living in the real world. New York, NY: Zondervan Publishing House, 1991.

Caner, Egun, Emir Caner. *Unveiling Islam: An Insider's Look at Muslim Life and Beliefs.* Grand Rapids, MI. Kregel Publications, 2002.

Cardwell, Jon J. *Christ and Him Crucified.* To Be A Pilgrim Press, 2011.

Clowney, Edmund P. *The Unfolding Mystery: Discovering Christ in the Old Testament.* Phillipsburg, NJ: P & R Publishing, 1988.

Copan, Paul and William Lane Craig. Passionate Conviction: *Contemporary Discourses on Christian Apologetics.* Nashville, TN: B&H Publishing Co., 2007.

Copan, Paul. *"True for You, But Not for Me." Deflating the Slogans that Leave Christians Speechless.* Bloomington, MN: Bethany House Publishers, 2010.

Cowan, Steven B., Gen. Editor. *Five Views on Apologetics.* Grand Rapids, MI: Zondervan, 2000.

Bibliography

Craig, William Lane & Joseph E. Gorra. *Answers to Tough Questions on God – Christianity and the Bible*. Chicago, IL: Moody Publishers, 2013.

Davis, Katie, Beth Clark. *Kisses from Katie*. New York, NY: Howard Books, 2011.

Deere, Jack. *Surprised by the Power of the Spirit*. Peabody, MA.: Hendrickson, 2003.

Dieter, Melvin E et al, *Five Views of Sanctification*. Grand Rapids, MI.: Zondervan, 1987.

Dobson, Dr. James. *Marriage Under Fire: Why We Must Win this Battle*. Sisters, OR: Multnomah Publishers, 2004.

Dobson, Dr. James. *The New Dare to Discipline*. Tyndale House Publishers, 1970, 1992.

Eggerichs, Dr. Emerson. *Love and Respect*. Nashville, TN: Thomas Nelson, Inc., 2004.

Ervin, Howard M. *Spirit Baptism: A Biblical Investigation*. Peabody, MA.: Hendrickson, 1987.

Farnell, F. David, Ed. *Vital Issues in the Inerrancy Debate*. Eugene, OR: Wipf and Stock Publishers, 2015.

Fee, G. D. *God's Empowering Presence: The Holy Spirit in the Letters of Paul*. Peabody, MA.: Hendrickson, 1994.

Fee, G. D. *Gospel and Spirit: Issues in New Testament Hermeneutics*. Peabody, MA.: Hendrickson, 1991.

Fee, G. D. *The First Epistle to the Corinthians*. The New International Commentary of the New Testament. Grand Rapids, MI.: Wm. B. Eerdmans, 1987.

Fee, Gordon D. *Paul's Letter to the Philippians*. Grand Rapids, MI. William B. Eerdmans Publishing Company, 1995.

Fu, Bob. *God's Double Agent*. Grand Rapids, MI.: Baker Books, 2013.

Geisler, David and Norman. *Conversational Evangelism: Connecting with People to Share Jesus*. Eugene, OR: Harvest House Publishers, 2014.

Geisler, Norman & William C. Roach. *Defending Inerrancy: Affirming the Accuracy of Scripture for a New Generation*. Grand Rapids, MI: Baker Books, 2011.

Geisler, Norman L. & David Farnell. *The Jesus Quest: The Danger from Within*. Xulon Press, 2014

Geisler, Norman L. & Frank Turek. *I Don't Have Enough Faith to be an Atheist*. Wheaton, IL: Crossway Books, 2004.

Geisler, Norman L. *Twelve Points that Show Christianity is True: A Handbook on Defending the Christian Faith*. Matthews, NC: Bastion Books, 2012.

Geisler, Norman. *Biblical Inerrancy: The Historical Evidence*. Matthews NC: Bastion Books, 1982, 2004, 2013.

Giglio, Louie. Goliath *Must Fall: Willing the Battle Against Your Giants*. Nashville, TN: W Publishing Group, 2017

Giglio, Louie. *The Comeback: It's Not Too Late You're Never Too Far*. Nashville, TN: W Publishing Group, 2015.

Graham, Billy. *Just As I Am: The Autobiography of Billy Graham*. HarperSanFrancisco & Zondervan, 1997.

Graham, Franklin. *Living Beyond the Limits: A Life in Sync with God*. Thomas Nelson, 1998.

Graham, Franklin. *Prayer for Revival, 80 Years Ago*. Billy Graham Evangelistic Assn., 2014.

Guinness, Os. *Impossible People: Christian Courage and the Struggle for the Soul of Civilization*. Downers Grove, IL: InterVarsity Press, 2016.

Hagee, John. *Jerusalem Countdown: A Warning to the World*. Lake Mary, FL. A Strang Company, 2006.

Harley, Jr., Willard F. *His Needs, Her Needs: Building an Affair-Proof Marriage*. Grand Rapids, Revell, 2010.

Harris, Sam. *The End of Faith: Religion, Terror, and the Future of Reason*. New York: W. W. Norton & Company, 2005

Henry, Carl. F. H. *God, Revelation and Authority*, Vols. 1-4. Word, Inc., 1979.

Hewer, C. T. R. *Understanding Islam: An Introduction*. Minneapolis, MN. Fortress Press, 2006.

Hitchcock, Mark. *Iran: The Coming Crisis. Radical Islam, Oil, and the Nuclear Threat*. Sisters, OR. Multnomah Publishers, 2006.

Hitchcock, Mark. *The Late Great United States: What Bible Prophecy Reveals About America's Last Days*. Colorado Springs, CO. Multnomah Books, 2009.

Horton, Stanley M. *I and II Corinthians*. A Logion Press Commentary. Springfield, Mo.: Gospel Publishing House, 1999.

Horton, Stanley M. *What the Bible Says about the Holy Spirit*. Springfield, MO.: Gospel Publishing House, 2005, 1976.

Hurlbut, Buck, *The Crucifixion of Jesu: Was it Really Friday?* No publisher indicated. Buck Hurlbut, 2020.

Hybels, Bill, Mark Middelberg. *Becoming a Contagious Christian* (Spanish edition). Grand Rapids, MI: Zondervan, 1994

Hybels, Bill. *Just Walk Across the Room: Simple Steps Pointing People to Faith*. Grand Rapids, MI: Zondervan, 2006.

Hybels, Bill. *The Power of a Whisper: Hearing God. Having the Guts to Respond*. Grand Rapids, MI.: Zondervan, 2010.

Hybels, Bill. *Too Busy NOT to Pray*. Downers Grove, IL: InterVarsity Press, 2008.

Igwe, Kate L. *Following Jesus Christ: Your Pathway to Effective Discipleship*. Xlibris Publishing Co., UK, 2014.

Ironside, H. A. *Philippians and Colossians*. Grand Rapids, MI: Kregel, 1920, 2007.

Jakes, T. D. *Destiny: Step into Your Purpose*. New York: FaithWords, 2015.

Jeremiah, David. *IS THIS THE END? Signs of God's Providence in a Disturbing New World*. Nashville, TN: W Publishing Group, 2016.

Jeremiah, David. *Prayer: The Great Adventure.* Colorado Springs, CO: Multnomah Books, 1997.

Jeremiah, Dr. David. *The Coming Economic Armageddon: What Bible Prophecy Warns about the New Global Economy.* New York. FaithWords, 2010.

Jeremiah, Dr. David. *What in the World is Going On?* Nashville, TN: Thomas Nelson, 2008.

Keller, Timothy. *Jesus the King: Understanding the Life and Death of the Son of God.* New York, NY. Penguin Random House, 2011.

Komoszewski, J. Ed, M. James Sawyer, Daniel B. Wallace. *Reinventing Jesus: How Contemporary Skeptics Miss the Real Jesus and Mislead*

Koop, C Everett, Schaeffer, Francis A., Whatever Happened to the Human Race? Wheaten, IL: Crossway Books, 1979.

Koukl, Gregory. *Tactics: A Game Plan for Discussing your Christian Convictions.* Grand Rapids, MI: Zondervan,

Landorf, Joyce. *what every woman wants in a man: tough & tender.* Old Tappan, NJ: Fleming H. Revell Co., 1975.

Langston, James. *America in Crisis: we have become the sum of our worst fears.* No publisher given, 2015.

Leman, Dr. Kevin. *The Birth Order Book: Why You Are the Way You Are.* Grand Rapids, MI: Revell, 1998.

Leman, Dr. Kevin. *The Firstborn Advantage: Making Your Birth Order Work for You.* Grand Rapids, Revell, 2008.

Lennox, John C. *God's Undertaker: Has Science Buried God?* Oxford, England: Wilkinson House, 2009.

Lewis, C. S. *Mere Christianity.* New York, NY: Harper Collins, 2001.

Lindsay, Hal. *The Late Great Planet Earth. Satan is Alive and Well on Planet Earth.* New York: Inspirational Press, 1970, 1977.

Lutzer, Erwin with Steve Miller. *The Cross in the Shadow of the Crescent: An Informed Response to Islam's War with Christianity.* Eugene, OR. Harvest House Publishers, 2013.

MacArthur, John. *The Lordship of Christ*. Nashville, TN: Thomas Nelson, 2012.

MacDonald, Gordon. *The Life God Blesses: Weathering the Storms of Life That Threaten the Soul*. Nashville, TN: Thomas Nelson Publishers, 1997.

Majors, Katie Davis. *Daring to Hope*. New York, NY: Multnomah, 2017.

Majors, Katie Davis. *Daring to Hope: Finding God's Goodness in the Broken and the Beautiful*. Colorado Springs, CO: Multnomah, 2017

Makary, Martin, and Ellen Vaughn. *Mama Maggie: the untold Story of One Woman's Mission to Love the Forgotten Children of Egypt's Garbage Slums*. Nashville, TN: Nelson Books, 2015.

Marshall, Catherine. *Something More*. Grand Rapids, MI.: Chosen Books, 2002.

Maxwell, John C. *Failing Forward: Turning Mistakes into Stepping Stones for Success*. Nashville, TN: Thomas Nelson, 2000.

Maxwell, L. E. *Crowded to Christ*. Grand Rapids, MI: Wm. B. Eerdmans, 1950

Mayhall, Jack and Carole: *Marriage Takes More than Love*. Colorado Springs, CO: NavPress, 1978.

McCarthy, Andrew C. *The Grand Jihad: How Islam and the Left Sabotage America*. New York, NY. Encounter Books,. 2010.

McGee, Robert S. *The Search for Significance*. Nashville, TN: Thomas Nelson, 2003.

McGrath, Alister E. *Mere Apologetics: How to Help Seekers & Skeptics Find Faith*. Grand Rapids, MI: Baker Books, 2012.

McManus, Erwin Raphael. *The Last Arrow: Save Nothing for the Next Life*. Colorado Springs, CO: WaterBrook, 2017.

McRay, John. *Paul: His Life and Teaching*. Grand Rapids, MI.: Baker Academic, 2003.

Michaels, J. Ramsey. New International Biblical Commentary: John. Pebody, Ma. Hendrickson Publishers, 1989.

Middelberg, Mark. *The Questions Christians Hope No One Will Ask.* Tyndale House Publishers, Inc., 2010.

Molina, Dr. Joaquin G. *What is Man?* Miami, Spring of Life Fellowship, 2013.

Montgomery, John Warwick. *God's Inerrant Word: An International Symposium on the Trustworthiness of Scripture.* Irvine, CA: NRP Books, 2015.

Moore, Frank. *Coffee Shop Theology: Translating Doctrinal Jargon into Everyday Life.* Kansas City: Beacon Hill Press, 1998.

Morgan, G. Campbell. *The Great Physician: The Method of Jesus with Individuals.* New York, NY: Fleming H. Revell Company, 1937.

Morgan, G. Campbell. *The Practice of Prayer.* New York, NY: Fleming H. Revell Company, 1906.

Morgan, G. Campbell. The Unfolding Message of the Bible: The Harmony and the Unity of the Scriptures. Westwood, NJ. Fleming H. Revell Company, 1961.

Morison, Frank. *Who Moved the Stone?* London, CrossReach Publications, 2016.

Myers, David G., and Jeeves, Malcolm A. Psychology Through the Eyes of Faith. New York, NY: Harper Collins, 2003.

Nee, Watchman. *The Spiritual Man.* New York, NY: Christian Fellowship Publishers, Inc., 1968.

Newman, Randy. *Questioning Evangelism: Engaging People's Hearts the Way Jesus Did.* Grand Rapids, MI: Kregel Digital Editions, 2010.

Panza, Christopher, Gale, Gale. *Existentialism for Dummies.* Hoboken, NJ: Wiley Publishing, Inc., 2008.

Pentecost, J. Dwight. *The Words and Works of Jesus Christ.* Grand Rapids, MI: The Zondervan Corporation, 1981.

Pickett, Fuchsia, *Cultivating the Gifts and Fruit of the Holy Spirit.* Book III, Lake Mary, Fl.: Charisma House Book Group, 2004.

Pink, Arthur W. *The Gospel of John* (Arthur Pink Collection Book 29).

Bibliography

Pink, Arthur W., *An Exposition of Hebrews*. Grand Rapids, MI: Baker Book House, 2004.

Pinnock, Clark H., Ed. *The Grace of God and the Will of Man*. Minneapolis, MN: Bethany House Publishers, 1989.

Piper, John. *Seeing and Savoring Jesus Christ*. Wheaton, IL: Crossway Books, 2001.

Pippert, Rebecca Manley. *Out of the Salt Shaker & into the World*. Downers Grove, IL.: InterVarsity Press, 1999.

Proctor, Bob. *12 Power Principles for Success*. Gildan Media, LLC., 2019.

Qureshi, Nabeel. *Seeking Allah, Finding Jesus*. Grand Rapids, MI: Zondervan, 2014.

Robinson, Jonathan. *Communication Miracles for Couples*. San Francisco, CA: Red Wheel/Weisser, LLC, 1997.

Rogers, Adrian. *Unveiling the End Times in Our Time*. Nashville, TN. Broadman & Holman Publishers, 2004.

Samples, Kenneth Richard. *7 Truths that Changed the World: Discovering Christianity's Most Dangerous Ideas*. Grand Rapids, MI: Baker Books, 2012.

Sandford, John Loren & Paula. *Restoring our Christian Family*. Lake Mary, FL: Charisma House, 2009.

Scroggie, W. Graham. *A Guide to the Gospels*. London: Pickering & Inglis, Ltd., 1952

Shank, Robert. *Life in the Son*. Springfield, MO: Westcott Publishers, 1960.

Shariathreat.com. *Sharia: The Threat to America: An exercise in Competitive Analysis: Report of Team B 11*. Washington, DC. Center for Security Policy, 2010.

Sheets, Dutch. *Intercessory Prayer*. Ventura, CA: Regal, 1996.

Sproul, R. C. *Defending Your Faith: An Introduction to Apologetics*. Wheaton, IL: Crossway Books, 2003.

Sproul, R. C. *reason to believe: a response to common objections to Christianity*. Grand Rapids, MI: Zondervan, 1982.

Sproul, R. C. *The Prayer of the Lord*. Orlando, FL: Reformation Trust Publishers, 2009.

Sproul, R. C. *The Work of Christ: What the Events of Jesus Life Means for You*. Colorado Springs, CO: David C. Cook, 2012.

Starnes, Todd. *Dispatches from Bitter America*. Nashville: B & H Publishing Group, 2012.

Starnes, Todd. *God Less America*. Lake Mary, FL: Charisma Media/Charisma House Book Group, 2014.

Stendal, Russell. *Rescue the Captors*. Life Sentence Publishing, 2011.

Stott, John. *Basic Christianity*. Downers Grove, IL: InterVarsity Press, 2008.

Stott, John. *Christ in Conflict*. Downers Grove, IL: InterVarsity Press, 2013.

Strickland, Danielle. *A Beautiful Mess: How God Re-creates Our Lives*. Grand Rapids, MI: Monarch Books, 2014.

Strobel, Lee. *The Case for Christ: A Journalist's Personal Investigation of the Evidence for Jesus*. Grand Rapids, MI: Zondervan, 1998.

Strobel, Lee. *The Case for Faith: A Journalist Investigates the Toughest Objections to Christianity*. Grand Rapids, MI: Zondervan, 2000.

Sumner, Tracy M., Ed. Th*e Essential Works of Andrew Murray*. Uhrichsville, OH: Barbour Publishing, 2008.

Swindoll, Charles. *Moses: A Man of Selfless Dedication*. Nashville, TN: W Publishing Group, a Division of Thomas Nelson, Inc., 1999.

Swindoll, Charles. *The Mystery of God's Will: What Does He Want For Me?* Nashville, TN: Word Publishing, 1999.

Tada, Joni Eareckson. *A Place of Healing: Wrestling with the Mysteries of Suffering, Pain, and God's Sovereignty*. Colorado Springs, CO: David C. Cook, 2010.

Tada, Ken and Joni Eareckson. *Joni & Ken: An Untold Love Story*. Grand Rapids, MI: Zondervan, 2013.

Bibliography

Taylor, Jack R. *Prayer: Life's Limitless Reach.* Nashville, TH: Broadman Press, 1977.

Thiessen, Henry Clarence. *Lectures in Systematic Theology.* Grand Rapids, MI: Wm. B. Eerdmans Publishing Company, 1949.

Thiselton, Anthony C. *First Corinthians: A Shorter Exegetical and Pastoral Commentary.* Grand Rapids, MI.: William B. Eerdmans Publishing Company, 2006.

Thomas, Gary. *Sacred Marriage.* Grand Rapids, MI: Zondervan, 2000.

Thomas, Gary. *Sacred Pathways: Discover Your Soul's Path to God.* Grand Rapids, MI. Zondervan, 2009

Wallas, Arthur. *Pray in the Spirit.* Fort Washington, PA: CLC Publications, 1970.

Willard, Dallas. *The Spirit of the Disciplines: Understanding How God Changes Lives.* New York, NY: Harper Collins, 1988.

Williams, David T. *Kenosis of God: The Self-limitation of God - Father, Son, and Holy Spirit.* Bloomington, IN: iUniverse, 2009.

Wright, N. T. *How God Became King: The Forgotten Story of the Gospels.* New York, NY: HarperCollins, 2011.

Wright, N. T. *Jesus and the Victory of God.* Minneapolis, MN: Fortress Press, 1996.

Wright, N. T. *Simply Jesus: A New Vision of Who He was, What He Did, and Why He Matters.* New York, NY: HarperCollins, 2011.

Wright, N. T. *Surprised by Hope.* New York, NY: HarperCollins Publishers, 2008.

Wright, N. T. Surprised by Hope: Rethinking Heaven, the Resurrection, and the Mission of the Church. New York, NY. HarperOne, 2008.

Wright, N. T. *The Challenge of Jesus: Rediscovering Who Jesus Was and Is.* Downers Grove, IL: InterVarsity Press, 1999.

Yancey, Philip. *Prayer: Does it Make any Difference?* Grand Rapids, MI: Zondervan, 2006.

Yancey, Philip. *Rumors of Another World: What on Earth are We Missing?* Grand Rapids, WI. Zondervan, 2003.

Yancey, Philip. *Vanishing Grace: What Ever Happened to the Good News?* Grand Rapids, MI: Zondervan, 2014.

Yong, Amos. *Who Is the Holy Spirit? A Walk with the Apostles.* Brewster, Mass.: Paraclete Press, 2011.

Young, Brad. H. *Jesus, the Jewish Theologian.* Grand Rapids, MI: Baker Academic, 2012.

Zacharias, Ravi & Norman Geisler, Gen. Editor. *Who Made God? And Answers to Over 100 Other Tough Questions of Faith.* Grand Rapids, MI: Zondervan, 2003.

Zacharias, Ravi. *Deliver Us from Evil.* Word Publishing, 2017.

Zacharias, Ravi. *The Grand Weaver: How God Shapes Us Through the Events of Our Lives.* Grand Rapids: Zondervan, 2007.

Zacharias, Ravi. *The Real Face of Atheism.* Grand Rapids, MI: Baker Books, 2004.

About the Author

The son of missionary parents, Larry Scott spent his formative years in Peru, living first in the city of Cusco before moving to Lima in 1951.

Following graduation from Central Bible College, Springfield, MO, with an AB degree in Bible, he spent a year in missionary service, teaching at the Assemblies of God Bible School in Santiago, Chile. Two years as Associate Pastor of Christ Church, Westminster, CA followed and then he moved to Camp Hill, Pa in 1968 and served as founding Pastor of Trinity Temple.

After ten years of ministry to the people of central Pennsylvania, he returned to academia to pursue an M Div. degree in Counseling from Ashland Seminary, Ashland, OH. Following graduation in 1982, and divorce in 1984, he virtually gave up on life, moved to Poulsbo, WA and lived a solitary life aboard Angelica, a 40-ft sailboat, in effect homeless, but garnering no sympathy. After fourteen years driving long-haul truck coast to coast, he retired in 2004 and remarried his sweetheart on what would have been their forty-fifth wedding anniversary. Together again, they sold Angelica, purchased a home, and moved to southern New Hampshire.

Now in a rebuilding mode, he has turned to writing, with *The Making of a Model* his crowning work.

This is not the story of failure due to drugs, alcohol, marital infidelity, or physical abuse. But this *is* the story of a man who made unbelievable mistakes and failed. But he stayed true to his calling, rose from the ashes of a shattered life, found a new sense of direction, and recovered ... living proof God can take even a broken man and make something special out of him — a living model of Jesus Christ.

Contact Larry

If you are interested in booking Larry to speak on any of the topics covered in this book, or for book signing events, he can be contacted by email at rlarryscott@gmail.com.

www.ingramcontent.com/pod-product-compliance
Lightning Source LLC
LaVergne TN
LVHW051111080426
835510LV00018B/1993